The
Digital Shield

AI in Cyber Defense

By
Drew Ashton

The Digital Shield

AI in Cyber Defense

Table of Contents

Introduction

In today's digitally-driven world, cybersecurity has become a pressing concern for individuals, businesses, and governments alike. Threats are constantly evolving, becoming more sophisticated and harder to detect. As we increasingly rely on technology for day-to-day operations and store vast amounts of sensitive data online, digital security becomes not just a priority but a necessity. In this context, Artificial Intelligence (AI) emerges as both a powerful ally and a transformative force.

The intersection of AI and cybersecurity offers a fascinating glimpse into the future of digital defense. AI technologies, including machine learning, deep learning, and natural language processing, are revolutionizing the way we approach cybersecurity. These advancements bring the promise of improved threat detection, faster response times, and even predictive capabilities that can anticipate attacks before they occur. This book aims to provide a comprehensive understanding of how AI is transforming cybersecurity, offering insights into the current technologies at play and future trends.

As cyber threats grow more complex, traditional methods of defense are no longer sufficient. Human analysts and conventional security systems struggle to keep up with the sheer volume and variety of attacks. Here, AI steps in, promising capabilities that were once the stuff of science fiction. From real-time monitoring systems to automated incident response, AI is reshaping the landscape of digital defense.

1

This book caters to a diverse audience that includes tech enthusiasts, cybersecurity professionals, and anyone interested in the evolving role of AI in cybersecurity. Whether you are new to the field or an experienced professional looking to deepen your understanding, this book aims to equip you with the knowledge to navigate this rapidly changing domain.

Our journey begins by exploring the historical context and early uses of AI in cybersecurity. Understanding the roots and initial applications helps us appreciate the rapid advancements and the key drivers behind AI's adoption in digital defense. We then delve into the various types of cyber threats, examining how they have evolved and why traditional defenses often fall short.

One of the most exciting aspects of AI in cybersecurity is its ability to process and analyze vast amounts of data—often in real-time. Techniques like machine learning and deep learning enable systems to recognize patterns and anomalies, flagging potential threats with unprecedented accuracy. These capabilities are crucial in an era where cyber adversaries are continually refining their methods to avoid detection.

In the chapters that follow, we will explore specific AI techniques and their applications in cyber defense. From anomaly detection to natural language processing, each technology plays a unique role in enhancing security measures. Real-world applications and case studies will illustrate how these technologies are being deployed effectively.

Threat detection is a critical component of any cybersecurity strategy. AI-powered systems can monitor network traffic, analyze user behavior, and detect intrusions more effectively than traditional systems. By leveraging AI, organizations can distinguish between normal and suspicious activities, reducing false positives and improving overall security posture.

Prevention is always better than cure, particularly in the realm of cybersecurity. AI aids in proactive defense mechanisms, predictive analytics, and automated patch management, ensuring vulnerabilities are addressed before they can be exploited. This proactive approach is essential to stay ahead of cyber adversaries who are constantly on the lookout for weaknesses to exploit.

Incident response is another area where AI shines. Automated incident response systems can significantly reduce the time it takes to contain and mitigate attacks. AI-driven forensics provide deeper insights into incidents, helping organizations understand the scope and impact of a breach. Effective crisis management relies on the ability to respond swiftly and accurately—capabilities that AI greatly enhances.

The role of big data in cybersecurity cannot be overstated. The ability to collect, store, and analyze massive datasets provides a wealth of information that can be harnessed for better security practices. However, dealing with such large volumes of data presents its own set of challenges, from storage and processing issues to privacy concerns. AI offers innovative solutions to these challenges, enabling more effective and efficient use of big data in cyber defense.

Cloud security is a major concern as more organizations migrate their operations to the cloud. AI offers robust solutions for securing cloud environments, identifying cloud-based threats, and ensuring compliance with security standards. Protecting data in the cloud is a complex task, requiring sophisticated tools that can adapt to the unique challenges presented by cloud infrastructures.

Ethical considerations and challenges are inherent in any discussion about AI and cybersecurity. Issues of bias, fairness, and privacy must be addressed to ensure that AI technologies are used responsibly. As we explore these challenges, it becomes clear that ethical AI is not just a goal but a necessity for the sustainable development of cybersecurity solutions.

Regulatory and legal aspects also play a crucial role in shaping the future of AI in cybersecurity. Understanding compliance requirements, global regulations, and the evolving landscape of cyber law is vital for organizations looking to leverage AI technologies. The legal framework must keep pace with technological advancements to provide guidelines and protections for both users and organizations.

Predicting the future is always challenging, but certain trends indicate the directions in which AI and cybersecurity are headed. Emerging technologies promise even greater advancements, and staying informed about these trends is essential for preparation and adaptation. This book will explore what the future holds for AI in cybersecurity and how we can prepare for tomorrow's threats.

By the end of this book, you will have a comprehensive understanding of how AI is transforming cybersecurity. You'll gain insights into current technologies, explore real-world applications, and confront the ethical and legal challenges that come with these advancements. Above all, you'll be better equipped to navigate the complex landscape of digital defense in the era of AI.

Let us embark on this journey to understand how AI is not just responding to the challenges of cybersecurity but actively shaping the future of digital defense.

Chapter 1:
The Rise of AI in Cybersecurity

The surge of artificial intelligence in cybersecurity represents a monumental shift in how we approach digital defense. Initially seen in experimental or niche applications, AI has now become a critical weapon in the cybersecurity arsenal. Key advancements in machine learning, deep learning, and natural language processing have been game-changers, enabling systems to detect and react to cyber threats with unprecedented speed and accuracy. These technologies are not just enhancing traditional defenses; they are transforming the cybersecurity landscape, allowing for predictive and adaptive measures that preemptively mitigate risks. As cyber threats evolve in complexity and sophistication, AI stands at the forefront, providing the agility and intelligence needed to defend against increasingly clandestine adversaries. This chapter delves into how AI started infiltrating the field of digital security and the pivotal factors driving its rapid adoption in the modern era.

Early Uses of AI in Digital Defense

When artificial intelligence (AI) began to intersect with cybersecurity, it brought a paradigm shift in how digital threats were managed. Back in the early days, AI was primarily utilized for straightforward tasks such as spam filtering and virus detection. These applications, though rudimentary by today's standards, set the stage for more sophisticated uses. Even simple rule-based systems demonstrated that algorithms could effectively aid in identifying and mitigating risks, leading IT professionals to invest further in AI research.

Spam filtering is one of the earliest and most quintessential implementations of AI in cybersecurity. By employing machine learning algorithms to analyze patterns in email content, AI systems could differentiate between spam and legitimate emails. This process involved classifying large datasets of emails into 'spam' and 'not spam' categories based on certain features such as the sender's address, email content, and subject line. Over time, these filters became more sophisticated, incorporating elements of natural language processing (NLP) to better understand the context and meaning of the email content.

Moving beyond spam detection, early AI systems were also deployed in antivirus software. Traditionally, antivirus programs relied on signature-based detection methods, which were effective but easily circumvented by new and evolving threats. AI stepped in to introduce behavior-based detection, which could identify potentially harmful actions by assessing a program's behavior rather than its known signature. This method allowed for the identification of new malware variants and provided a more robust defense mechanism against previously unknown threats.

In addition to these consumer-facing applications, early AI technologies found utility in the enterprise sector as well. Intrusion Detection Systems (IDS), for instance, leveraged AI to monitor network traffic and identify unusual patterns that might indicate a cyber attack. Machine learning models were trained using historical data to distinguish between normal and malicious behaviors. These systems could then provide real-time alerts, enabling quicker responses to potential security incidents. Compared to the manual monitoring processes of the past, AI-driven IDS represented a significant leap forward in efficiency and effectiveness.

As AI technologies developed, so did their applications in more complex areas like anomaly detection. Initially, rule-based systems, which required substantial manual input and constant updating, were the norm. However, the integration of AI allowed for more dynamic and adaptive systems. Anomaly detection algorithms started learning normal patterns of behavior within a network and flagged anything that deviated from these patterns as potential threats. This approach was particularly useful in identifying zero-day attacks, where traditional signature-based systems fell short.

Picture a typical large organization with thousands of employees, devices, and applications generating log data continuously. Sifting through this data manually for security threats would be a Herculean task. Early AI applications addressed this by automating data analysis processes, capable of processing and scrutinizing vast amounts of information rapidly. These AI systems could spot irregularities, such as unauthorized access attempts or unusual data transfers, and alert human analysts who could then investigate further.

Another significant early use of AI in digital defense was in the realm of predictive analytics. Using historical data and machine learning models, organizations began to predict potential vulnerabilities and attacks before they occurred. This capability was crucial for adopting a proactive rather than reactive security posture. By analyzing past incidents and identifying commonalities and trends, AI could forecast future threats, providing invaluable insight to cybersecurity teams.

However, integrating AI into digital defense wasn't without its challenges. One of the earliest hurdles was the quality and quantity of data required to train machine learning models effectively. In the beginning, data was often sparse, unstructured, and riddled with noise, making accurate predictions difficult. Over time, as more data became available and data processing technologies improved, the effectiveness of AI models in cybersecurity also saw a marked increase. High-quality, curated datasets allowed for more accurate training, resulting in better performance of AI systems in detecting and mitigating threats.

Moreover, AI's early implementation in cybersecurity often necessitated a collaborative approach. Hybrid systems that combined AI capabilities with human oversight became prevalent. These systems capitalized on AI's speed and pattern recognition abilities while leveraging human intuition and expertise for final decision-making. This symbiotic relationship between AI and human analysts formed the bedrock of many advanced cybersecurity systems we see today.

Early adopters of AI in digital defense also had to contend with skepticism and resistance from within the industry. Many cybersecurity professionals were wary of relying heavily on AI, concerned about the technology's potential inaccuracies and the implications of false positives or negatives. Despite these reservations, the consistent success of AI in various preliminary applications built trust and laid the groundwork for more widespread acceptance and integration of AI technologies in cybersecurity ecosystems.

Finally, it's essential to acknowledge the role of early AI cybersecurity experiments in shaping regulatory and ethical standards. As AI began to demonstrate its capabilities in digital defense, policymakers and industry leaders started to consider the ethical implications of deploying autonomous systems in making critical security decisions. Issues like data privacy, the potential for algorithmic bias, and the need for transparency in AI decision-making processes came to the forefront. These considerations have informed the development of regulatory frameworks that guide the responsible use of AI in cybersecurity.

The pioneering efforts in leveraging AI for spam filtering, anomaly detection, predictive analytics, and other early applications have been instrumental in defining the trajectory of AI in digital defense. These initial steps have not only proven AI's potential to revolutionize cybersecurity but have also provided invaluable lessons that continue to shape current and future developments in this ever-evolving field.

In summarizing the formative years of AI in digital defense, it's evident that these early applications were crucial in demonstrating the technology's utility and laying the groundwork for more advanced innovations. The journey from simple spam filters to sophisticated, adaptive security systems highlights the transformative power of AI. These early endeavors have set the stage for a future where AI plays an indispensable role in safeguarding our digital world.

Key Drivers of AI Adoption

Artificial Intelligence (AI) has swiftly become a cornerstone in cybersecurity, driven by its capacity to analyze, adapt, and respond to threats faster and more efficiently than traditional methods. The global surge in cyber threats, the increasing complexity of attacks, and the ever-expanding digital landscape have necessitated advancements in defense mechanisms. AI is not just a reaction to these challenges but a fundamental shift in how organizations approach network security.

One of the primary drivers of AI adoption in cybersecurity is the sheer scale and velocity of cyber threats. Each day, cybersecurity professionals confront millions of potentially malicious activities, from phishing attempts to intricate malware attacks. Traditional human-centric approaches, while still valuable, are simply no match for this overwhelming volume. AI, with its capability to sift through vast amounts of data and identify anomalies in real-time, offers a remedy that is both scalable and robust.

Another crucial factor is the sophistication of modern cyber attacks. Gone are the days when viruses and malware were easily detectable through signature-based systems. Today's threats are often polymorphic and can morph to evade detection. AI excels here by employing advanced machine learning and deep learning techniques that go beyond signature-based detection. It can recognize patterns and behaviors that signal potential threats, even if these threats have never been encountered before.

The expanding digital ecosystem also plays a significant role. With the proliferation of Internet of Things (IoT) devices, cloud computing, and mobile technologies, the attack surface for cyber criminals has widened. Organizations now grapple with securing not just traditional IT infrastructure but an interconnected array of devices and platforms. AI's adaptability makes it particularly suited for this complex landscape, where it can manage and secure a diverse array of endpoints with minimal human intervention.

In addition, regulatory pressures and compliance requirements are encouraging the adoption of AI in cybersecurity. Industries such as finance, healthcare, and critical infrastructure must adhere to stringent regulations to protect sensitive data. Non-compliance can result in hefty fines and reputational damage. AI helps organizations maintain compliance by continuously monitoring for vulnerabilities and automating remediation processes, thus ensuring that security protocols are always up-to-date and compliant.

Cost efficiency is another compelling driver. Although initial investments in AI technologies can be substantial, the long-term savings in terms of reduced labor costs and mitigated breaches are significant. AI systems can operate around the clock without fatigue, handling tasks that would otherwise require large teams of cybersecurity experts. This not only reduces operational costs but also frees up human resources to focus on more strategic initiatives.

Furthermore, the rise of AI in consumer technology has established a level of comfort and expectation around its capabilities. From virtual assistants to personalized recommendations, AI's integration into daily life has demystified the technology. This growing comfort with AI solutions provides a smoother transition when these technologies are adapted for use in cybersecurity.

AI's ability to provide predictive analytics is also crucial. By analyzing historical data, AI can forecast potential threats, allowing organizations to take a proactive stance rather than a reactive one. This shift from reactive to proactive defense is a game-changer, enabling the anticipation and neutralization of threats before they materialize, thus considerably reducing the risk and impact of cyber attacks.

Another significant driver is the inadequacy of traditional cybersecurity measures in the face of zero-day vulnerabilities. Zero-day attacks exploit previously unknown vulnerabilities, catching traditional defenses off guard. AI, with its learning and adaptive capabilities, can recognize and respond to these threats more effectively than static security models. By continuously learning from new data and experiences, AI can identify and mitigate the impact of zero-day vulnerabilities more efficiently.

Moreover, the integration of AI in cybersecurity is driven by the need for automated threat response. Manual intervention is not just slow but also prone to errors, which can be costly in a high-stakes environment. AI-powered systems can automate the detection and response processes, reducing the time taken to neutralize threats and minimizing human error. This rapid response is crucial in minimizing the damage from cyber attacks.

The shortage of skilled cybersecurity professionals further fuels the adoption of AI. With a global talent gap, many organizations struggle to find the expertise needed to manage complex security challenges. AI helps alleviate this shortage by augmenting the capabilities of existing teams, enabling them to handle more with less. Augmented intelligence, where AI and human experts work in tandem, is becoming a standard approach in the industry.

In summary, the adoption of AI in cybersecurity is driven by multiple interrelated factors. The increasing scale and complexity of cyber threats, the necessity for cost-effective and efficient solutions, the expanding digital ecosystem, regulatory requirements, the need for predictive analytics, the inadequacy of traditional methods against zero-day vulnerabilities, the demand for automated threat response, and the global shortage of cybersecurity talent all contribute to AI's growing presence in this field. As AI continues to evolve, its role in digital defense will undoubtedly become even more pivotal, shaping the future of cybersecurity in profound ways.

Chapter 2:
Understanding Cyber Threats

In the ever-evolving landscape of cybersecurity, grasping the various cyber threats is paramount for defense strategies to be effective. Cyber threats have become increasingly sophisticated, targeting both individual users and large-scale organizations with varying methodologies and objectives. Malware and ransomware, for instance, are engineered to infiltrate systems, encrypt data, and demand payment, often leaving victims paralyzed. Meanwhile, phishing and social engineering attacks exploit human vulnerabilities, tricking individuals into divulging sensitive information. Advanced Persistent Threats (APTs) represent a more insidious form of attack, where persistent and stealthy tactics are employed to gain long-term access to high-value information. The nature of cyber attacks is continuously evolving, with attackers adopting innovative techniques to circumvent traditional defenses. Understanding these threats is not just about recognizing their existence but also about analyzing their behaviors and intentions. This evolving threat landscape necessitates the adoption of sophisticated defense mechanisms, many of which are now being powered by artificial intelligence, to stay one step ahead.

Types of Cyber Threats

Understanding cyber threats is crucial to developing effective defenses, especially with the rapid evolution of Artificial Intelligence in cybersecurity. Cyber threats come in various forms, including malware and ransomware that aim to disrupt or take control of systems for financial gain. Phishing and social engineering attacks exploit human vulnerabilities, often tricking individuals into revealing confidential information. Advanced Persistent Threats (APTs) represent a more sophisticated category where attackers infiltrate systems over long periods, aiming to steal sensitive data without detection. These threats are continually evolving, making it imperative to stay updated on the latest tactics and countermeasures. A comprehensive grasp of these threat types lays the groundwork for implementing AI-driven solutions to enhance cybersecurity measures.

Malware and Ransomware have consistently posed severe threats to cybersecurity, and with the advent of AI, both the offensive and defensive landscapes have evolved dramatically. For starters, malware designed to infiltrate and damage systems has become more sophisticated. These malicious programs can outmaneuver traditional detection mechanisms, exhibiting behavior that mimics legitimate software. On the other side, ransomware, a form of malware that locks victims out of their data until a ransom is paid, has exploded in prevalence, targeting not just individuals but also corporations and critical infrastructure.

AI has transformed the way we approach the detection and prevention of these digital menaces. Traditional methods of identifying malware often relied on signature-based detection. This involves matching patterns in data to known malware signatures, which is effective when the malware is already documented. However, it falls short with new and unknown threats. The dynamic nature of modern cyberattacks requires a correspondingly dynamic approach. Here, AI, especially machine learning algorithms, can shine by recognizing malware based on its behavior rather than a set signature.

Machine learning models can analyze vast amounts of data to identify patterns indicative of malware activities. These models are trained on diverse datasets comprising known malware behaviors and benign activities. This training allows them to predict when a piece of software is acting suspiciously, even if it doesn't match any existing signatures. Consequently, these AI models can detect zero-day attacks—new and previously unknown vulnerabilities exploited by malware—much more effectively than traditional methods.

Deep learning, a subset of machine learning, pushes these capabilities further. With deep learning, models can process and analyze unstructured data, such as logs, network traffic, and even user actions, to identify malware behavior. These models use neural networks with multiple layers that can understand the high-level abstract features of malicious activities. Thus, deep learning-based systems offer a higher detection accuracy, reducing false negatives and enabling more robust protection.

Similarly, ransomware has evolved to become more insidious, employing advanced techniques to avoid detection and encryption of victim data. Traditionally, ransomware attacks begin with spear-phishing emails containing malicious attachments or links. Once the victim clicks on the attachment or link, the ransomware installs itself on the system. Modern ransomware, however, uses sophisticated encryption methods and can propagate across networks, leveraging AI mechanisms to navigate through defenses.

AI-powered defenses can counter ransomware by analyzing behavior patterns specific to ransomware attacks. For instance, AI systems can monitor file access patterns and detect anomalies consistent with the mass encryption of files. When these anomalies are detected, the systems can swiftly isolate infected machines, preventing the ransomware from spreading and encrypting further data. AI's ability to provide real-time analysis and response is crucial in mitigating the effects of ransomware attacks.

Behavioral analysis, enabled by AI, is vital for identifying ransomware before it causes significant harm. By continuously learning from each threat it encounters, an AI system can improve its predictive capabilities. Integrating these AI models with real-time monitoring systems enhances their ability to act on detected anomalies instantly. In some cases, AI can even roll back changes made by ransomware, restoring encrypted files from shadow copies or backups.

Anomaly detection, another key AI technique, helps in recognizing both malware and ransomware. By establishing a baseline of what constitutes "normal" behavior within a network or on a host, anomaly detection models can identify deviations that indicate potential threats. This proactive approach allows for the early identification and mitigation of suspicious activities before they evolve into full-blown attacks. Through continuous learning, these models adapt to evolving threats, becoming more effective over time.

Moreover, AI's application in threat intelligence gathering is invaluable. AI systems can scour multiple sources—dark web forums, threat databases, and security feeds—to gather and analyze intelligence on new and emerging malware and ransomware threats. This intelligence aids in preemptive defense measures and informs the training of AI models, making them better equipped to recognize novel threats.

The automation provided by AI is another game-changer in the battle against malware and ransomware. Automated systems can handle the voluminous data involved in modern cybersecurity, sifting through it to identify and respond to threats at speeds unattainable by human analysts. This automation extends to incident response systems, where AI can take immediate actions such as isolating infected systems, deploying patches, and notifying cybersecurity teams.

Developing and deploying AI-based cybersecurity tools isn't without its challenges. One significant hurdle is ensuring that these tools do not introduce new vulnerabilities. AI models need robust training datasets to function effectively, and if these datasets are compromised or biased, they can lead to incorrect threat assessments. Secure, diverse, and representative data collection is therefore essential to developing reliable AI threat detection models.

Interpreting AI decisions adds another layer of complexity. While AI can flag a potential threat, understanding the why behind that judgment is crucial for cybersecurity professionals. Transparency in AI algorithms, often referred to as explainable AI, ensures that the decisions made by these systems can be comprehended and scrutinized. This transparency is critical for building trust in AI solutions and ensuring that they augment human decision-making rather than replacing it.

Overall, combating malware and ransomware in the age of AI involves a blend of advanced technology and human oversight. AI's ability to detect, analyze, and respond to threats in real-time fundamentally enhances our defense mechanisms. Yet, it is the collaboration between human expertise and AI's capabilities that offers the most effective strategy in cybersecurity. Moving forward, continuous innovation and adaptation will be vital in staying ahead of increasingly sophisticated cyber threats.

As AI continues to evolve, so too will the tactics of cybercriminals. It will be essential to maintain a proactive and vigilant approach, leveraging the latest advancements in AI to secure our digital environments. The cat-and-mouse game between defenders and attackers sees no end, but with AI on our side, the balance of power increasingly shifts towards robust, resilient defense.

Phishing and Social Engineering are among the most insidious forms of cyber threats that exploit human psychology rather than technical vulnerabilities. The essence of these attacks lies in their manipulation of trust and deceit to achieve their malicious goals. Whether it's a cleverly crafted email that appears to be from a trusted source or a more direct phone call, the endgame often remains the same: to trick individuals into divulging sensitive information or to unwittingly install malware on their systems. The rise of sophisticated AI technologies has transformed both the execution and the defense mechanisms against these attacks.

At its core, phishing involves impersonation. Attackers often pretend to be someone you know or trust—a colleague, a bank, or even a popular online service. They use this facade to trick you into providing sensitive information like passwords, credit card numbers, or other personal details. Traditional phishing emails might have been riddled with obvious grammatical errors, but today's AI-powered phishing schemes can be eerily convincing. Language models can generate text that's almost indistinguishable from a legitimate message, bypassing many of the older detection techniques that relied on spotting linguistic anomalies.

Social engineering extends beyond mere email interactions. Phone calls, social media interactions, and even face-to-face encounters can be avenues for these malicious attempts. Attackers leverage social psychology principles to gain trust, such as authority, urgency, and reciprocity. Imagine receiving a call from someone claiming to be your IT department, urgently requesting you reset your password due to an ongoing system issue. It's a classic example of social engineering, exploiting the urgency to lower your guard.

Artificial Intelligence serves a dual role in the landscape of phishing and social engineering: it's a tool both for attackers and defenders. On the offensive side, AI can analyze large datasets to craft highly personalized phishing attacks. By scraping social media profiles and other publicly available information, AI algorithms can generate messages that resonate more personally with the recipient. For example, you might receive an email referencing a recent event you attended, making the communication appear more legitimate and relevant. This level of personalization increases the likelihood of a successful compromise.

Conversely, AI is a powerful ally in identifying and mitigating these threats. Machine Learning (ML) algorithms can be trained on vast datasets of known phishing emails and other forms of social engineering attempts to recognize patterns and anomalies indicative of malicious intent. They can evaluate various indicators such as the sender's email domain, the linguistic style of the message, and even the URLs embedded within. By cross-referencing this data with known malicious patterns, AI systems can flag suspicious communications before they reach the intended target.

Behavioral analysis is another AI-driven technique employed to counteract social engineering. By establishing a baseline of normal user behavior, AI can detect deviations indicative of a compromised account. For instance, if an employee who typically accesses the company servers from a specific IP address suddenly logs in from an unfamiliar location or attempts to download large volumes of data, the system can trigger an alert for further investigation. This proactive approach helps in catching incidents early before a significant breach occurs.

The integration of Natural Language Processing (NLP) into cybersecurity frameworks further enhances the ability to detect subtler forms of social engineering. NLP can parse through the textual content of communications to identify sentiment, intent, and context. It can detect subtle discrepancies and unusual prompts that may suggest an impersonation attempt. For instance, if an email requests sensitive information in an uncharacteristic tone or manner, NLP can flag this for review. This capability is invaluable for organizations dealing with high volumes of emails and messages daily, where manual scrutiny would be infeasible.

Despite these advancements, the arms race between attackers and defenders is ongoing. As AI-driven defenses improve, so too do the techniques employed by malicious actors. One emerging trend is the use of Deepfakes in social engineering attacks. Using advanced neural networks, attackers can create realistic video and audio impersonations, tricking victims into believing they are interacting with a real person. For example, a deepfake video of a CEO instructing an employee to wire funds to a fraudulent account carries a high potential for success due to the convincing nature of the deception.

Organizations must also emphasize education and training as a crucial line of defense against phishing and social engineering. AI can assist in designing more effective training programs by simulating realistic attack scenarios. Employees can be exposed to AI-generated phishing emails in a controlled environment, allowing them to learn from their mistakes without the associated risks. Additionally, AI can analyze the results of these training exercises, identifying areas where employees are particularly vulnerable and need additional guidance.

Creating a culture of skepticism and vigilance is vital for mitigating the risks associated with social engineering. Encouraging employees to verify the authenticity of unusual requests, especially those involving sensitive information or financial transactions, adds another layer of security. Multi-factor authentication (MFA) can further protect against compromised credentials, making it more challenging for attackers to gain unauthorized access even if they succeed in stealing log-in details.

AI's role in combating phishing and social engineering will continue to evolve, driven by ongoing research and innovation. Future advancements may include even more sophisticated anomaly detection algorithms, real-time speech and video analysis to counter deepfake technology, and AI-powered personal digital assistants that can screen communications and warn users of potential risks. However, it is crucial to remember that technology alone cannot solve these challenges. A comprehensive approach combining AI-driven solutions, user education, and robust organizational policies will be necessary to stay ahead of ever-evolving cyber threats.

In conclusion, phishing and social engineering remain significant threats in the digital realm, exploiting human behavior to achieve malicious ends. While AI has empowered attackers with more sophisticated tools, it also offers robust defensive capabilities to detect and prevent such attacks. By leveraging AI technologies alongside continuous education and vigilance, organizations can significantly reduce the risks associated with these deceptive practices, safeguarding their assets and maintaining trust in a digital age.

Advanced Persistent Threats (APTs) are a category of cyber threats distinguished by their sophistication and persistence. Unlike conventional attacks, which often aim for quick hits, APTs are all about the long game. Hackers executing APTs are not in a rush; they infiltrate a network quietly, maintaining their foothold over an extended period to extract maximum data and cause substantial damage. These attackers often form part of well-funded groups, sometimes state-sponsored, leveraging an arsenal of advanced tools and techniques.

What's particularly worrying about APTs is their strategic intent. The goal is usually to extract sensitive information rather than cause immediate disruption. This could range from intellectual property theft to acquiring confidential state documents. Because of the high stakes, APTs tend to target high-profile organizations including governments, research institutions, and large corporations. They typically employ a multi-phase strategy: initial infiltration, establishing a backdoor, expanding their control, harvesting data, and finally, exfiltration.

The initial breach often exploits zero-day vulnerabilities or highly sophisticated phishing attacks. Once inside, the attackers install a backdoor, a type of malware that allows them ongoing access to the network. Subsequently, the attackers work on elevating their privileges within the system to avoid detection and to move laterally across the network. This lateral movement is where APTs stand out; they methodically map the network, identify key data, and operate stealthily to avoid triggering any alarms.

Advanced Persistent Threats are a different beast altogether because they're adaptive. These attackers monitor the organization's response to their presence and alter their tactics accordingly. If a backdoor is discovered and closed, they will likely have several other hidden accesses in place. This game of cat and mouse can go on for months, or even years, making it immensely challenging for cybersecurity professionals to eliminate the threat completely.

Artificial Intelligence (AI) is increasingly proving to be a game-changer in combating APTs. Traditional cybersecurity measures rely heavily on predefined rules and behavior signatures, which APTs can easily circumnavigate by being unpredictable and adaptive. AI, on the other hand, offers the ability to learn and adapt much like the attackers. Machine learning algorithms can analyze vast amounts of data and identify patterns that signify an APT. For instance, unusual login times, peculiar data transfer patterns, or odd application behavior could all be indicators of an APT lurking within the network.

However, the sophistication of APTs demands more than just anomaly detection. Deep learning models add another layer of robustness by understanding complex patterns and behaviors that might not be obvious or linear. These models can develop a contextual understanding of what constitutes 'normal' behavior for different segments of the network and highlight any deviations that could suggest an APT. Natural Language Processing (NLP) applications can even scan email communications and documents to detect phishing attempts or embedded malicious codes aiming for the initial breach.

Another compelling approach involves AI-driven threat hunting. This proactive method turns the tables on APTs, identifying them in the reconnaissance stage itself. AI threat hunters continuously scan the network, looking for any hallmarks of an APT before it establishes a strong foothold. The integration of AI in Security Information and Event Management (SIEM) systems improves the speed and accuracy of detecting and responding to APTs, providing cybersecurity teams with actionable insights and recommendations in real time.

Yet, even with AI, combating APTs is an arms race. The same technologies employed for defense can also be weaponized by attackers. For example, cybercriminals can use AI to refine their social engineering tactics or to develop adaptive malware that automatically changes its signature to avoid detection. This makes it essential for cybersecurity experts to stay ahead of the curve, leveraging AI not just reactively, but proactively to anticipate and thwart potential APTs.

To further complicate matters, APTs are evolving. They now incorporate advanced techniques such as fileless malware, which resides in the memory rather than on the hard disk, rendering traditional anti-malware tools ineffective. They also make use of encryption and secure deletion to cover their tracks, making forensic investigations extremely challenging. AI and Machine Learning (ML) models have to keep pace, constantly evolving their methods to track and counter these new tactics.

Organizations must also focus on endpoint security, utilizing AI-powered Endpoint Detection and Response (EDR) systems. These systems can monitor and analyze activity at endpoints, identify potential threats in real-time, and even autonomously respond to mitigate risks. The key to managing APTs lies in a layered security approach. Combining network security, endpoint security, and continuous monitoring enabled by AI ensures that even if one line of defense is breached, others stand guard to prevent further damage.

Collaboration between AI-driven systems and human expertise is vital. While AI can handle the bulk data analysis and detect anomalies at scale, human analysts bring in the contextual understanding and intuition that AI currently lacks. This symbiotic relationship fortifies an organization's defense mechanisms, making them more resilient against the sophisticated barrage of APTs.

Moreover, integrating AI in incident response can drastically cut down on response times. Swiftly isolating affected segments of the network, initiating forensics, and implementing recovery protocols are crucial to limiting the damage caused by an APT. AI's ability to automate these processes while learning from each incident makes the organization better prepared for future threats.

In conclusion, while Advanced Persistent Threats represent one of the most formidable challenges in the cybersecurity landscape, the integration of AI offers a potent countermeasure. From initial detection to adaptive defensive maneuvers and incident response, AI bolsters an organization's ability to withstand these sophisticated attacks. As AI technologies continue to evolve, they promise to tip the scales in favor of cyber defense, ensuring that organizations remain one step ahead in this ongoing battle.

The Evolving Nature of Cyber Attacks

The landscape of cyber attacks has dramatically shifted over the years, presenting a continuous challenge to cybersecurity experts. In the early days, attackers primarily focused on relatively simple and isolated exploits—like basic malware or standalone viruses. Today, however, cyber threats have grown exponentially more complex and multifaceted, representing a dynamic arena where tactics constantly evolve in response to emerging defense mechanisms. As technology advances, so too does the sophistication of cyber attacks, often employing the latest advancements in AI and machine learning to outsmart traditional security measures.

One of the most compelling signs of the evolving nature of cyber attacks is the increasing prevalence of Advanced Persistent Threats

(APTs). These are highly sophisticated, long-term campaigns that are often state-sponsored. They aim to infiltrate and remain within systems for extended periods, extracting valuable information unnoticed. Unlike traditional threats that may cause immediate damage, APTs prioritize stealth and persistence, subtly manipulating or surveilling data over months or even years. The intricate nature of APTs exemplifies the lengths to which attackers will go to achieve their objectives.

Phishing schemes and social engineering tactics have also become alarmingly more advanced. What was once limited to poorly worded emails asking for personal information has evolved into highly targeted, well-researched attacks. Cybercriminals now utilize social media and other publicly available information to personalize their phishing efforts, making them more convincing and difficult to detect. These sophisticated tactics manipulate the natural trust that users have in reputable sources, compromising credentials and sensitive information with alarming efficiency.

Ransomware attacks remain a constant and growing threat. In recent years, we've seen a shift from opportunistic attacks on individuals to targeted attacks on large organizations, including municipalities, health institutions, and even critical infrastructure. These attacks have evolved to not only encrypt data but also to exfiltrate it, threatening to leak sensitive information unless the ransom is paid. Such strategies amplify the pressure on victims, increasing the likelihood of ransom payments and raising the stakes for organizational cybersecurity defenses.

The proliferation of Internet of Things (IoT) devices has introduced a new frontier for cyber attacks. With billions of interconnected devices now in use, from smart home systems to industrial control systems, each new device represents a potential entry point for malicious actors. Many of these devices suffer from insecure default configurations and lack robust security updates, making them vulnerable to exploitation. The challenge is compounded by the interconnected nature of these devices, where vulnerabilities in one can provide a foothold for a broader network compromise.

Another critical aspect of the evolving cyber threat landscape is the increasing use of AI by cyber attackers themselves. Machine learning algorithms can be employed to automate and scale attacks far beyond what was previously possible. For instance, AI can be used to quickly identify system vulnerabilities, craft highly personalized phishing emails, or even develop new strains of malware that can adapt and evade detection. This adversarial use of AI signifies a dangerous arms race in cybersecurity, where defenders and attackers are continually trying to outdo one another using the latest technological advancements.

Supply chain attacks are another area of growing concern. In these attacks, cyber criminals target less-secure elements within a supply chain to compromise the entire system. By focusing on third-party vendors or partners who might have weaker security protocols, attackers can eventually gain access to more secure targets. These types of attacks highlight the interconnected risks in modern digital ecosystems, where the security posture of one entity can significantly impact others.

In addition to these evolving tactics, attackers are increasingly leveraging encryption to cloak their activities. While encryption is essential for protecting legitimate data, it can also be used by malicious actors to hide command and control communications, data exfiltration, and other nefarious activities. This dual-use nature of encryption creates a significant challenge for cybersecurity professionals tasked with monitoring and detecting potential threats without violating users' privacy.

Cryptojacking is a relatively new phenomenon in the world of cyber attacks. It involves unauthorized use of someone else's computing resources to mine cryptocurrencies. While it may seem less damaging than data theft or ransomware, cryptojacking can seriously degrade system performance and render critical operations inefficient. The rising value of cryptocurrencies has only incentivized attackers to develop more sophisticated methods for embedding cryptomining scripts in unsuspecting victims' systems.

The evolution in cyber attacks has prompted a corresponding evolution in defense strategies. Traditional signature-based detection methods are often inadequate against these sophisticated, rapidly changing threats. As a result, there is a significant shift towards behavioral analytics and anomaly detection, powered by AI. These newer methods don't rely solely on known patterns of malicious activity. Instead, they assess normal behaviors and flag deviations, making it more difficult for attackers to slip by unnoticed.

Finally, artificial intelligence itself is a double-edged sword in the context of cybersecurity. While AI-powered tools are indispensable for modern threat detection and response, the same technologies can be repurposed for offensive strategies. This cyclical nature of technological advancement necessitates a proactive and adaptive approach to cybersecurity. We are entering an era where continuous learning, agile defense mechanisms, and an in-depth understanding of adversarial tactics are not just beneficial but essential for staying ahead of threats.

Understanding the evolving nature of cyber attacks is crucial for developing comprehensive defense strategies. As we've explored, cyber threats have grown more sophisticated, diverse, and covert. To counteract these threats effectively, cybersecurity measures must also evolve, embracing cutting-edge technologies while staying vigilant against the continually shifting tactics of malicious actors. Whether through AI-driven defense mechanisms or innovative user education programs, the fight against cyber attacks requires a multi-faceted and ever-adaptive approach.

Chapter 3:
AI Techniques in Cyber Defense

The integration of artificial intelligence into cybersecurity strategies has brought about a new era in digital defense. Machine learning, for instance, excels at recognizing patterns and can adapt to new threats by continually learning from vast datasets. Deep learning, a subset of machine learning, pushes this further with neural networks that can simulate human-like decision-making processes, offering unprecedented accuracy and speed in threat detection. Natural language processing (NLP) empowers systems to understand and counteract phishing attempts and social engineering by analyzing and interpreting human language in emails, messages, and other forms of communication. Furthermore, anomaly detection leverages AI to identify deviations from standard user or system behavior, flagging potential threats that might bypass traditional security measures. With these AI techniques, cybersecurity becomes not just reactive but proactively anticipates, identifies, and mitigates risks in real-time, enhancing the overall resilience of digital infrastructures.

Machine Learning

Machine learning (ML) has swiftly become a cornerstone in the universe of cyber defense, transforming the way organizations detect, analyze, and mitigate threats. Its adaptability and ability to derive insights from vast datasets have made it indispensable for contemporary cybersecurity strategies. Unlike traditional rule-based systems, which require exhaustive and continual updates, machine learning models learn from data. They evolve, improving their detection capabilities as they are exposed to more information. This dynamic learning process enhances the resilience of cyber defenses against emerging threats.

One of the primary ways machine learning is leveraged in cyber defense is through the development of models that can identify and classify different types of cyber threats. By training on extensive datasets containing known examples of malware, phishing attempts, and other types of cyber attacks, these models can discern patterns and anomalies that indicate malicious activity. Supervised learning, a common ML technique where models are trained on labeled data, is frequently employed here. The model ingests datasets that include both malicious and benign samples, learning to differentiate between the two with increasing accuracy.

Unsupervised learning, another critical machine learning approach, excels in scenarios where labeled data isn't available. By analyzing patterns and relationships within the data, unsupervised models can detect anomalies that deviate from the norm. These anomalies often signal emerging threats that have not yet been categorized or understood. This capability is particularly vital in an ever-evolving threat landscape where novel attack vectors frequently appear.

In addition to anomaly detection, machine learning algorithms are instrumental in behavioral analysis. By continuously monitoring user and network behavior, ML models establish a baseline of "normal" activity. Any deviation from this baseline may trigger an alert, allowing cybersecurity teams to investigate potential breaches or insider threats. The intricacies of this process underscore the importance of having precise, data-driven insights to inform security measures.

Moreover, reinforcement learning, a more advanced form of machine learning, has found its place in cybersecurity. By creating a simulated environment where models can learn from trial and error, reinforcement learning algorithms optimize security protocols and responses to threats. This autonomous learning mechanism mirrors the way living organisms learn from their surroundings, making it a powerful tool in the cybersecurity arsenal.

Let's talk about the role of deep learning within the broader machine learning ecosystem. While detailed deep learning techniques are beyond this section's scope, it is important to note that deep learning models offer remarkable precision in recognizing and responding to complex threat patterns. These models utilize neural networks with numerous layers, processing vast amounts of data to uncover even the most elusive cyber threats. Their ability to self-improve as they process more data adds an invaluable layer of depth to cyber defense strategies.

Feature engineering is another crucial component of machine learning in cybersecurity. The process involves selecting and transforming data attributes that will be most effective for a given machine learning model. In cybersecurity contexts, features might include network traffic patterns, user login times, or file access behaviors. Effective feature engineering can significantly enhance a model's capability to detect threats accurately and efficiently.

One of the critical factors in the success of machine learning models in cybersecurity is the quality and quantity of the data they are trained on. Data must be diverse and representative of various types of legitimate and malicious activities. However, acquiring high-quality data can be challenging due to the sensitive nature of cybersecurity incidents and concerns over privacy and confidentiality. Despite these hurdles, organizations can utilize synthetic data generation techniques and data anonymization to build robust datasets that fuel their ML models.

Scalability is another key advantage of machine learning in cyber defense. In large-scale environments, where massive amounts of data are generated, traditional cybersecurity measures can become overwhelmed. Machine learning models, however, can process and analyze data at a scale and speed unattainable for human analysts. This scalability ensures that defenses remain robust and relevant in the face of growing cyber threats.

Additionally, machine learning's ability to integrate seamlessly with other AI techniques, such as Natural Language Processing (NLP) and anomaly detection, further augments its utility in cybersecurity. By combining various AI techniques, organizations can build more sophisticated and layered defense mechanisms that address a broader spectrum of cyber threats. This interdisciplinary approach amplifies the effectiveness and adaptability of cybersecurity strategies.

However, it's essential to understand that the deployment of machine learning models isn't a one-time effort. These models need regular updates and retraining to account for new types of attacks and evolving threat landscapes. Continuous learning is vital, and organizations must invest resources in ensuring their ML models remain up-to-date and effective. Automation can assist in this area, employing algorithms that schedule periodic retraining sessions based on the latest data.

Machine learning also plays a critical role in augmenting threat intelligence. By analyzing data from various sources such as threat feeds, logs, and past incidents, ML models can identify emerging trends and predict potential future attacks. Predictive analytics, powered by machine learning, enable organizations to prepare proactive defense measures, mitigating risks before they manifest. This foresight is invaluable in staying ahead of cyber adversaries.

Collaboration between human experts and machine learning systems represents another critical frontier in cyber defense. While ML models excel at processing and identifying patterns within large datasets, human analysts bring contextual understanding and creativity, enhancing decision-making processes. By working in tandem, human-machine teams can tackle complex cybersecurity challenges more effectively than either could alone.

The growing importance of machine learning in cybersecurity is evident, but its integration is not without challenges. One significant concern is the potential for adversarial attacks, where cybercriminals manipulate input data to deceive machine learning models. Ensuring the robustness and security of ML models against such attacks is a pressing area of research. Organizations must employ techniques such as adversarial training and model hardening to safeguard their machine learning-based systems.

Ethical considerations also come to the fore with the deployment of machine learning in cyber defense. Issues such as bias in training data can lead to skewed outcomes, disproportionately affecting specific groups or individuals. Ensuring fair and impartial ML models requires a conscientious approach to data collection, processing, and validation. Transparency in how these models operate and the decisions they make is equally vital to maintain trust and accountability.

In summary, machine learning has fundamentally reshaped the landscape of cyber defense. Its capabilities, ranging from anomaly detection and behavioral analysis to predictive analytics, offer unparalleled advantages in safeguarding digital environments. While challenges and ethical considerations must be navigated, the potential for machine learning to enhance and transform cybersecurity strategies is immense. As cyber threats continue to evolve, so too will the machine learning techniques that defend against them, ensuring a dynamic and responsive approach to digital security.

Deep Learning

Deep learning has become an integral part of modern cybersecurity, primarily due to its ability to analyze vast amounts of data and identify complex patterns that traditional algorithms might miss. Unlike machine learning models, which often require feature engineering and expert knowledge to decide which data features to use, deep learning models automatically extract relevant features from raw data. This capability is powered by neural networks, particularly deep neural networks, which consist of multiple layers that mimic the human brain's structure and functioning.

One of the key advantages of deep learning in cyber defense is its proficiency in handling unstructured data. Whether it's network traffic logs, emails, or social media posts, unstructured data is abundant and often contains valuable insights. Convolutional Neural Networks (CNNs) and Recurrent Neural Networks (RNNs) are particularly useful. CNNs excel at identifying patterns in visual data, making them suitable for image recognition tasks, such as identifying malicious code snippets in software binaries. On the other hand, RNNs are adept at processing sequential data, which is essential for tasks like analyzing user behavior over time to detect anomalies.

The practical applications of deep learning in cybersecurity are myriad. For instance, deep learning models are highly effective in identifying phishing attacks. By training on a diverse dataset of phishing and legitimate emails, these models can discern subtle cues that indicate whether an email is a phishing attempt. Similarly, deep learning can enhance malware detection. Traditional signature-based methods often fail to detect new malware variants, but deep learning models can identify suspicious behaviors and code segments that suggest the presence of malware.

Moreover, deep learning can significantly improve intrusion detection systems (IDS). By continuously learning from network traffic and user behavior, these models can identify deviations that might indicate an intrusion. This capability is particularly beneficial for identifying zero-day attacks, where no prior knowledge of the threat exists. In such scenarios, the ability to detect unusual patterns becomes crucial.

Another compelling aspect of deep learning in cyber defense is its role in predictive analytics. Predictive models can forecast future attacks based on historical data. For example, by analyzing patterns in past cyberattacks, deep learning algorithms can predict the likelihood of future threats and inform proactive defense strategies. This foresight allows organizations to allocate resources more effectively and patch vulnerabilities before they can be exploited.

However, deploying deep learning in cybersecurity isn't without challenges. One significant hurdle is the requirement for large datasets to train models effectively. Acquiring and labeling such data can be resource-intensive. Moreover, deep learning models are computationally intensive and may require specialized hardware, such as GPUs, to perform efficiently. These factors can be prohibitive for smaller organizations with limited resources.

Additionally, the interpretability of deep learning models remains a contentious issue. While these models are highly effective, their decision-making processes can be opaque. This opacity raises concerns in cybersecurity, where understanding why a model flagged a particular event as malicious is essential. Explainable AI (XAI) techniques are emerging to address this issue, aiming to make deep learning models more transparent and their decisions easier to understand.

Despite these challenges, the integration of deep learning into cybersecurity continues to advance. Research in adversarial machine learning, for instance, explores how attackers might deceive deep learning models and how to defend against such tactics. By understanding these adversarial techniques, researchers can develop more robust models that can withstand sophisticated cyberattacks.

Another exciting area of development is the combination of deep learning with other AI techniques. For example, natural language processing (NLP) can be integrated with deep learning to enhance the analysis of textual data, such as chat logs or security incident reports.

This synergy can provide more comprehensive insights and improve the overall effectiveness of cybersecurity measures.

Finally, as deep learning continues to evolve, its role in cybersecurity will likely expand. Emerging technologies, such as federated learning, offer promising avenues for collaborative defense strategies. Federated learning allows models to be trained across multiple organizations without sharing sensitive data, enhancing privacy and security while leveraging the collective intelligence of the community.

In conclusion, deep learning represents a powerful tool in the arsenal of cybersecurity professionals. Its ability to process and analyze vast amounts of data, detect anomalies, and predict future threats makes it indispensable in the ongoing battle against cyber adversaries. However, it's crucial to navigate the associated challenges, such as data requirements and model interpretability, to harness its full potential. As deep learning techniques continue to advance, they will undoubtedly play a pivotal role in shaping the future of cyber defense.

Natural Language Processing (NLP)

In the intricate dance of cyber defense, Natural Language Processing (NLP) emerges as a formidable player, transforming how cybersecurity professionals interpret and respond to digital threats. NLP, a branch of artificial intelligence, equips machines with the ability to understand, interpret, and generate human language. Within the sphere of cybersecurity, it offers profound abilities to dissect vast troves of unstructured text data, transforming them into actionable insights.

NLP's role in cyber defense is inherently tied to its ability to process and analyze textual data. In an industry teeming with logs, alerts, emails, and numerous other text-based forms of communication, NLP techniques help sift through this data, identifying potential threats with unprecedented speed and accuracy. Essentially, NLP acts as the linguistic interpreter in the cybersecurity team's toolkit, enabling machines to understand the context and intent behind human language.

Consider phishing emails, one of the most common and persistent cyber threats. Traditional defenses might flag emails based on known malicious signatures or keywords, but sophisticated phishing attempts often bypass these rudimentary checks. NLP, however, can analyze the nuanced language used within an email, understanding context, sentiment, and intent. By spotting anomalies in the language patterns, NLP tools can flag potential phishing attempts even if they haven't been encountered before, thus offering a dynamic layer of defense.

The growing complexity of Advanced Persistent Threats (APTs) also underscores the importance of NLP in cyber defense. APTs often employ various social engineering tactics to infiltrate organizations. Here, NLP's ability to understand and analyze language patterns becomes crucial. By examining patterns in communication—whether internal emails or external messages—NLP can help identify and mitigate these threats before they escalate.

Natural Language Processing in Incident Response

Beyond detecting threats, NLP significantly amplifies incident response capabilities. During and after a cyber attack, vast amounts of data generated can overwhelm human analysts. NLP streamlines this process by quickly parsing through logs, incident reports, and threat intelligence feeds. By automatically categorizing and prioritizing incidents based on linguistic patterns, NLP allows cybersecurity teams to respond more swiftly and effectively.

A critical application of NLP in incident response is the automated generation of reports. Immediate, accurate documentation of incidents is paramount for post-incident analysis and prevention of similar future attacks. NLP facilitates the extraction of key details from various communications and logs, compiling them into coherent reports that capture the essence of the incident without inundating analysts with superfluous information.

Behavioral Analysis through Language Patterns

Another compelling application of NLP in cyber defense is its role in behavioral analysis. Cyber threat actors often betray themselves through subtle linguistic cues in their communication. NLP models can be trained to recognize these cues, distinguishing between typical user behavior and potentially malicious activities. This extends to analyzing code comments, documentation, and other forms of textual data that might contain intent or context clues about the nature of the software.

Furthermore, the integration of NLP with machine learning models enhances predictive capabilities. By continuously learning from new data, NLP models can adapt and evolve, staying a step ahead of cyber threats. The combination of historical data and real-time analysis empowers these systems to predict and neutralize threats more accurately.

Challenges and Limitations

Despite its advantages, NLP in cyber defense is not without challenges. Language is inherently complex and ambiguous. The subtleties of sarcasm, idiomatic expressions, and evolved slang can pose significant hurdles for NLP algorithms. Moreover, context-sensitive interpretation is critical; the same phrase might be benign in one context but malicious in another. This necessitates continuous refinement and training of NLP models to maintain their efficacy in diverse scenarios.

The dynamic nature of cyber threats also means that NLP models require regular updates. Cybercriminals constantly evolve their tactics, using new jargon and phrases to circumvent detection. Keeping NLP systems up-to-date with these changes is an ongoing endeavor, requiring collaboration between cybersecurity experts and linguists.

Integration with Other AI Techniques

NLP does not operate in isolation; its true potential in cyber defense is unleashed when integrated with other AI techniques, such as machine learning and deep learning. For instance, NLP can feed processed text data into machine learning models, improving the precision of threat detection algorithms. Deep learning enhances this further, enabling the analysis of more complex and abstract language patterns.

Incorporating NLP into anomaly detection systems also augments their accuracy. By discarding the noise and focusing on linguistic anomalies, these systems can better identify deviations from normal behavior. The synergy between NLP and other AI techniques creates a multi-layered defense strategy that is robust, adaptive, and resilient.

The Future of NLP in Cybersecurity

Looking ahead, the evolution of NLP promises even greater advancements in cyber defense. As AI technology advances, we can expect NLP to become more sophisticated, understanding context with greater nuance and less data. The future holds the possibility of real-time language processing, where systems can detect and respond to threats as they occur, providing a critical advantage in the fast-paced world of cybersecurity.

Moreover, advancements in NLP could lead to more intuitive and human-like interactions between security systems and analysts. This could make cybersecurity tools more accessible, reducing the barrier to entry for new professionals and democratizing the field. The convergence of NLP with emerging technologies like quantum computing and neuromorphic engineering could further redefine the landscape of digital defense.

In conclusion, Natural Language Processing is a cornerstone of modern cybersecurity strategies. Its ability to parse, analyze, and interpret human language equips cybersecurity professionals with tools to combat evolving threats effectively. While challenges persist, the continuous integration of NLP with other AI technologies heralds a future where digital defense is proactive, intelligent, and adaptive. By leveraging the power of language understanding, NLP ensures that our defenses evolve as rapidly as the threats we face.

Anomaly Detection

In the realm of cyber defense, the role of anomaly detection is indispensable. Trained to spot deviations from the norm, anomaly detection systems serve as the digital sentinels, continuously scanning for irregular activities that may indicate a breach, an attack, or other malicious behaviors. As cyber threats continue to evolve in sophistication and frequency, the importance of robust anomaly detection mechanisms can't be overstated. Leveraging Artificial Intelligence (AI) and Machine Learning (ML), these systems have become pivotal in identifying patterns that would be imperceptible to even the most experienced human analysts.

Traditionally, cybersecurity relied heavily on signature-based detection methods. These methods, while effective to some extent, had their limitations. They required prior knowledge of the threat to detect it. In contrast, anomaly detection doesn't bank on predefined signatures. Instead, it utilizes AI to understand what constitutes normal behavior within a network and flags any deviation from that norm. This shift from a reactive to a more proactive approach marks a significant evolution in cybersecurity strategies.

Machine Learning algorithms play a critical role in anomaly detection. These algorithms sift through massive amounts of data, learning the intricacies of network traffic, user behaviors, and system operations. By continually refining their understanding of what "normal" looks like, they become adept at spotting anomalies, even those that don't match any known threats. This capability is particularly crucial in defending against zero-day exploits, which are attacks that take advantage of previously unknown vulnerabilities.

Deep Learning, a subset of Machine Learning, offers additional advantages. It employs neural networks with multiple layers (hence, 'deep') to analyze complex patterns in data. These networks can discern subtle anomalies that simpler algorithms might miss. For instance, a deep learning model can differentiate between legitimate user access and an attacker mimicking that user's behavior, even if the latter closely resembles the former.

Natural Language Processing (NLP) aids in anomaly detection by parsing human language in communication channels and logs. It can analyze emails, chat logs, and other text-based communications to identify phishing attempts, social engineering attacks, and other text-based threats. NLP algorithms can flag unusual activities, such as a sudden change in the tone or frequency of communication, which may be indicative of an impending attack.

Anomaly detection in cybersecurity isn't limited to identifying potential threats. It also plays a significant role in incident response. By detecting anomalies, systems can trigger automated responses, such as isolating affected devices, rerouting traffic, or alerting security personnel. This rapid response can significantly reduce the damage caused by attacks, minimizing downtimes and safeguarding sensitive data.

Behavioral analysis is an essential component of anomaly detection. It examines the typical behavior of users, devices, and applications within a network. By establishing a baseline of normal activities, behavioral analytics can detect deviations that may indicate the presence of malicious actors. For example, if a user's access patterns suddenly change, such as logging in from a different geographic location or accessing unusual resources, the system flags this as an anomaly.

However, the effectiveness of anomaly detection systems isn't absolute. False positives, where benign activities are flagged as threats, remain a challenge. These false alarms can lead to alert fatigue among security personnel, causing genuine threats to be overlooked. AI models need continuous training and fine-tuning to minimize false positives while maintaining a high detection rate. This balance is difficult to achieve but crucial for the success of anomaly detection systems.

Incorporating feedback loops into anomaly detection systems can significantly enhance their effectiveness. When a flagged activity is confirmed as a threat or deemed benign, this information feeds back into the AI model, helping it learn and improve its accuracy over time. This iterative process ensures that the detection system becomes more adept at distinguishing between normal and malicious activities, reducing the occurrence of false positives and negatives.

Moreover, the integration of anomaly detection with other cybersecurity measures fosters a more comprehensive defense strategy. For instance, combining anomaly detection with Intrusion Detection Systems (IDS) can provide a multi-layered security approach. While IDS might focus on known attack patterns and signatures, anomaly detection can cover the gaps by identifying previously unknown threats based on behavior changes.

Real-time monitoring is another critical aspect of anomaly detection. Continuous surveillance allows systems to promptly identify and respond to anomalies. In heavily regulated industries, where compliance and security are paramount, real-time monitoring ensures that any deviation is quickly flagged and addressed, minimizing potential damage and adhering to regulatory requirements.

Nonetheless, it's essential to recognize the limitations and challenges associated with anomaly detection in cybersecurity. One significant challenge is the vast amount of data that needs to be processed. As networks grow and more devices connect to the internet, the volume of data generated increases exponentially. Handling such massive datasets requires significant computational power and advanced algorithms capable of processing and analyzing data efficiently.

Despite these challenges, the future of anomaly detection in cybersecurity looks promising. Advances in AI and ML continue to enhance the capabilities of anomaly detection systems. Developing more sophisticated algorithms, improving computational resources, and refining the understanding of normal behavior within networks are key areas of ongoing research and development. These efforts are driving the evolution of anomaly detection, ensuring it remains a vital component of cybersecurity.

Furthermore, the intersection of anomaly detection with other emerging technologies presents exciting possibilities. For instance, integrating anomaly detection with Blockchain technology could enhance transparency and integrity in detecting anomalies. Blockchain's immutable ledger would ensure that detected anomalies and subsequent actions are recorded in a tamper-proof manner, increasing trust in the detection and response processes.

In conclusion, anomaly detection stands as a cornerstone in the digital fortress of cybersecurity. By leveraging advanced AI techniques, it offers a proactive approach to identifying and mitigating threats. While challenges remain, the continuous evolution of AI technologies promises to refine and enhance anomaly detection systems further. As cyber threats become more sophisticated, the importance of anomaly detection in fortifying digital defenses will only continue to grow.

Chapter 4:
AI in Threat Detection

In the ever-evolving landscape of cybersecurity, using AI for threat detection stands out as a game-changing advantage. Leveraging real-time monitoring systems, AI enables unprecedented visibility into network activities, flagging anomalies that could indicate potential threats. By continuously analyzing behavior patterns, AI identifies deviations that may signal an impending breach or ongoing attack. This chapter will delve into various intrusion detection systems (IDS) enhanced by AI, breaking them down into network-based and host-based categories. These sophisticated systems go beyond traditional rule-based detection, using machine learning algorithms to recognize even the most subtle indicators of compromise. The proactive nature of AI-driven threat detection ensures that organizations can quickly respond to and mitigate risks, safeguarding vital digital assets in an increasingly hostile cyber environment.

Real-Time Monitoring Systems

In the ever-evolving landscape of cybersecurity, real-time monitoring systems have become indispensable. They serve as the vigilant sentinels, always on guard, ensuring that any abnormal activity is flagged and investigated immediately. Unlike the traditional methods, which often relied on periodic checks and manual interventions, real-time monitoring leverages artificial intelligence to provide continuous, proactive defense. This paradigm shift is critical in countering the sophisticated and increasingly frequent cyber threats we face today.

At the heart of real-time monitoring systems lies the capability to process vast amounts of data in milliseconds. With the sheer volume of data that enterprises deal with, it's humanly impossible to keep track of every packet of information manually. AI-driven systems, however, excel at this task. By employing machine learning algorithms, these systems can understand and recognize patterns of normal behavior. Once the baseline is established, any deviation, no matter how minute, is promptly flagged for further inspection.

The beauty of AI in real-time monitoring is its ability to learn and evolve. For instance, a network traffic spike at odd hours might initially trigger an alert. However, if the system learns that this spike is due to an automated backup or a global team's work hours, it can adjust its parameters accordingly. This reduces false positives, which are a significant challenge in cybersecurity, allowing security teams to focus on genuine threats.

Furthermore, the integration of anomaly detection with real-time monitoring adds another layer of sophistication. Anomaly detection uses AI to sift through historical data and identify what 'normal' looks like. It doesn't just rely on predetermined rules but uses statistical models to detect abnormalities. Combined with real-time monitoring, this provides a potent toolset to identify and mitigate threats instantaneously.

In addition to these functionalities, the scalability of real-time monitoring systems makes them suitable for organizations of all sizes. Whether it's a small business or a multinational corporation, the ability to scale the monitoring process ensures that cybersecurity measures grow in tandem with the organization. This scalability is especially crucial in industries like finance or healthcare, where the stakes are particularly high.

Real-time monitoring isn't just about defense; it also facilitates rapid response and recovery. Upon detecting a threat, immediate actions can be taken—ranging from isolating affected systems to initiating incident response protocols. This rapid intervention is pivotal in minimizing damage and ensuring business continuity. A case in point is the swift action taken during Distributed Denial of Service (DDoS) attacks. Real-time monitoring systems can instantly reroute traffic, deploy mitigation strategies, and notify the relevant personnel, preventing extensive service outages.

One significant advantage of these systems is their capacity to integrate seamlessly with other security tools. Intrusion Detection Systems (IDS), Security Information and Event Management (SIEM) tools, and even endpoint security solutions can all feed data into and receive alerts from real-time monitoring platforms. This interconnected ecosystem allows for a more comprehensive security posture, ensuring that no aspect of digital defense is overlooked.

Behavior analysis is another key feature of real-time monitoring systems. By continuously analyzing user and entity behavior, these systems can detect potential insider threats, which are notoriously difficult to identify. For example, if a user suddenly accesses sensitive data or deviates significantly from their usual patterns, the system can flag this as suspicious. Coupled with machine learning, this behavior analysis becomes more precise over time, minimizing false alerts and focusing on genuine anomalies.

The employment of Natural Language Processing (NLP) further enriches real-time monitoring capabilities. NLP can be used to analyze logs and communications, identifying potential threats hidden in plain sight. For instance, phishing attempts often contain subtle cues that traditional systems might miss. NLP can parse through emails, chat logs, and other text-based communications to detect these cues, adding another layer of protection.

With cyber-attacks becoming more sophisticated, leveraging big data in real-time monitoring is not just advantageous but essential. By collecting and analyzing data from various sources in real-time, these systems can build a broader picture of potential threats. This helps in identifying patterns that might indicate a coordinated attack strategy. The role of big data analytics cannot be overstated, as it provides the context necessary for making informed, rapid decisions.

Moreover, AI in real-time monitoring systems enables predictive analytics. This involves using historical data and trends to anticipate future threats. For example, if a certain type of malware is spreading in a particular industry, predictive analytics can forecast its potential impact on your organization. This allows for preemptive measures, offering a proactive instead of reactive approach to cybersecurity.

It's also important to acknowledge the challenges associated with real-time monitoring systems. One major issue is the need for a robust infrastructure to handle the data processing requirements. Real-time monitoring can generate a significant amount of data, and processing this data swiftly requires both powerful hardware and efficient algorithms. Additionally, the constant evolution of cyber threats means that these systems need continuous updates to remain effective.

Another challenge lies in the potential for alert fatigue. Even with machine learning to reduce false positives, security teams can still face an overwhelming number of alerts. Effective real-time monitoring systems incorporate prioritization mechanisms to tackle this problem. By categorizing alerts based on their severity and potential impact, these systems help ensure that the most critical threats are addressed first.

Despite these challenges, the benefits of real-time monitoring systems far outweigh the drawbacks. They provide a level of agility and responsiveness that is crucial in today's fast-paced cyber threat landscape. The ability to detect, analyze, and respond to threats in real-time can be the difference between a minor incident and a catastrophic breach.

In terms of future developments, we can expect real-time monitoring systems to become even more sophisticated. With advancements in AI and machine learning, these systems will be able to predict threats with greater accuracy, adapt to new types of attacks more swiftly, and integrate more seamlessly with other cybersecurity tools. The incorporation of edge computing could further enhance the speed and efficiency of data processing, making real-time monitoring even more effective.

In conclusion, real-time monitoring systems represent a critical component of modern cybersecurity strategies. Their ability to provide continuous oversight, adapt to new threats, and integrate with a wide range of other security tools makes them indispensable. As cyber threats continue to evolve, so too will these systems, ensuring that they remain at the forefront of digital defense.

Behavior Analysis

Behavior analysis stands as a vital pillar in the realm of AI-driven threat detection. It leverages artificial intelligence to scrutinize and understand the behavioral patterns of users, systems, and network entities. Unlike traditional methods that primarily rely on static rule-based systems, behavior analysis introduces a dynamic approach to identifying threats by recognizing deviations from the norm.

At the heart of behavior analysis is the concept of baselining. This involves creating a comprehensive profile of what constitutes "normal" behavior for a given entity. Through continuous monitoring, AI systems establish a baseline by observing routine activities, typical network traffic, and standard user behavior. Any deviation from this baseline is flagged as anomalous, warranting further investigation. This method significantly enhances the detection of emerging threats that slip past conventional signature-based defenses.

Understanding and identifying user behavior is crucial in thwarting insider threats. Unlike external attacks, insider threats originate from within the organization and are notoriously difficult to detect. By employing advanced machine learning algorithms, AI systems can profile individual user behavior patterns over time. Sudden access to sensitive files, unusual login times, or attempts to exfiltrate data can be detected early, alerting security teams to potential malfeasance.

Furthermore, behavior analysis isn't just limited to human users. It extends to devices and systems, ensuring a holistic security posture. For instance, a dormant server suddenly initiating outbound connections to unfamiliar IP addresses may signal a compromise. AI-powered behavior analysis tools can spot these anomalies in real time, allowing for swift remediation.

One of the principal advantages of using AI for behavior analysis in threat detection is its adaptability. Traditional systems necessitate manual updates to stay relevant against ever-evolving threats, but AI models can learn and adapt autonomously. This continuous learning process enables the systems to keep pace with new attack vectors and tactics used by cyber adversaries.

However, it's not just about detecting anomalies. The true power of AI lies in its ability to discern between benign irregularities and genuine threats. For instance, an employee accessing the network during unusual hours might simply be working late. AI systems, trained on vast datasets, can differentiate between innocent deviations and actions that represent a threat, reducing false positives and ensuring that security teams can focus their efforts on genuine risks.

The integration of natural language processing (NLP) into behavior analysis further enriches threat detection. By parsing and understanding communications, AI can identify suspicious language patterns or unusual data requests that might indicate a phishing attempt or a spear-phishing campaign. This capability enhances the detection of social engineering attacks, which often rely on deceptive and sophisticated language to trick users into revealing sensitive information.

A critical facet of behavior analysis is its role in protecting against advanced persistent threats (APTs). These threats are characterized by prolonged and targeted attacks, often spearheaded by organized cybercriminal groups or nation-states. APTs meticulously evade traditional detection methods by blending in with normal network traffic. By constantly monitoring and analyzing behavior patterns, AI can uncover the subtle signs of an APT, such as the gradual accumulation of privileges or lateral movement across the network.

Collaborative filtering is another technique employed in behavior analysis. Drawing parallels from recommendation systems used in e-commerce, AI analyzes behavior across a multitude of users or entities to identify patterns indicative of potential threats. If a particular command sequence or transaction pattern typically precedes a security breach, the system can flag similar occurrences in real time, providing early warnings and insights.

Behavior analysis also plays a pivotal role in compliance and regulatory adherence. Organizations are increasingly required to demonstrate due diligence in monitoring and safeguarding against threats. By maintaining detailed logs and analyses of behavior patterns, AI-driven systems provide the requisite evidence of proactive threat management, helping organizations stay compliant with industry standards and regulations like GDPR, HIPAA, and others.

It's equally important to address the potential challenges that come with behavior analysis. The sheer volume of data generated in modern networks can be overwhelming. Effective behavior analysis requires robust data processing capabilities and sophisticated analytics to sift through and interpret massive datasets. Fortunately, advances in big data technologies and cloud computing have made it feasible to handle these demands efficiently.

Moreover, the effectiveness of behavior analysis depends heavily on the quality and comprehensiveness of the data fed into the system. Incomplete or biased data can skew the baseline and lead to inaccurate threat detection. Therefore, ensuring data integrity and coverage is paramount. This often involves integrating information from various sources, including logs, application data, and network traffic, to build a cohesive and accurate behavioral profile.

Behavior analysis is not a silver bullet. It's part of a broader, multifaceted approach to cybersecurity that includes anomaly detection, signature-based detection, and heuristics. Together, these methods create a robust defensive stance, capable of addressing a wide array of threats. However, behavior analysis does stand out for its proactive nature, focusing on identifying and addressing threats before they can execute malicious activities.

The role of AI in behavior analysis continues to evolve, with research and development driving new capabilities and enhancements. Future advancements may see deeper integration of AI with behavioral biometrics, enriching the analysis further by incorporating physiological and behavioral characteristics unique to individuals, such as typing patterns or mouse movements.

In conclusion, behavior analysis represents a significant leap forward in the capabilities of threat detection systems. By leveraging AI to scrutinize and understand both user and system behaviors, it's possible to identify and address threats that might otherwise go unnoticed. As cyber threats evolve, so too must our defenses, and behavior analysis offers a promising avenue for maintaining a proactive and resilient cybersecurity posture.

Intrusion Detection Systems (IDS)

Intrusion Detection Systems (IDS) represent a vital echelon in the hierarchy of AI-driven threat detection methods, acting as the sentinels of our digital fortresses. By leveraging advanced machine learning algorithms, AI-enhanced IDS can both detect and respond to unauthorized access attempts or malicious activities within a network or host environment. Unlike traditional systems that rely heavily on predefined signatures of known threats, AI-powered IDS employ anomaly detection techniques to identify unusual patterns that may indicate novel or sophisticated cyber attacks. Furthermore, these systems continuously evolve by learning from new threats, thereby improving detection accuracy over time. As cyber threats become more complex and sneaky, the role of AI in augmenting IDS becomes increasingly indispensable, ensuring robust, adaptive defenses that go beyond mere reactive measures.

Network-Based IDS play a critical role in contemporary cybersecurity frameworks, offering a layer of defense that's both formidable and flexible. Often abbreviated as NIDS, these systems monitor network traffic for suspicious activity, helping identify and mitigate potential cyber threats before they cause significant damage. Their operation hinges on the capability to analyze vast amounts of data in real-time, which has become increasingly feasible with advancements in artificial intelligence (AI) and machine learning.

To understand the architecture of NIDS, it's important to first grasp how these systems intercept and scrutinize data packets traversing a network. Much like a vigilant security guard, NIDS continuously assess network traffic at multiple points, scanning for anomalies or known threat patterns. Traditionally, this involves deep packet inspection (DPI), a process that examines the content of data packets rather than just their headers. By evaluating both the source and destination, alongside the payloads, NIDS can detect abnormalities indicative of various attack vectors, such as malware, unauthorized access attempts, or data exfiltration.

With AI-infused NIDS, the capabilities of these systems are significantly enhanced. AI models, especially those based on machine learning and deep learning algorithms, can analyze traffic patterns with unparalleled precision. This level of scrutiny enables the detection of both known and unknown threats (often referred to as zero-day threats). Machine learning models can be trained on historical traffic data, learning to distinguish between benign and malicious activities. Over time, these systems become adept at identifying subtle deviations from normal behavior, quickly flagging potential intrusions.

Real-time monitoring is perhaps one of the most potent features of AI-driven NIDS. Traditional systems often rely on predefined rule sets or signature-based detection, which can be slow to adapt to new threats. In contrast, AI systems utilize anomaly detection methodologies that can dynamically adapt to evolving threat landscapes. This ensures that even novel attacks, which haven't been previously encountered, can be detected and mitigated in real-time. This capability is indispensable in today's fast-paced digital environment, where attackers continuously refine their tactics to evade detection.

Moreover, the integration of Natural Language Processing (NLP) within NIDS can further amplify their effectiveness. By analyzing command and control (C2) communications in various payloads or network traffic, NLP algorithms can detect malicious intent or abnormal communication patterns. For example, if an unusually high number of outgoing requests to command and control servers is detected, the system can flag this as an indicator of potential botnet activity. This multi-faceted approach to threat detection, combining different AI techniques, makes modern NIDS a robust defense mechanism.

However, the deployment of AI-enhanced NIDS isn't without its challenges. One of the primary issues is the sheer volume of data that needs to be processed. In large organizational networks, the amount of traffic can be staggering, necessitating high computational power and advanced data processing capabilities. AI can help mitigate this by using efficient algorithms and parallel processing techniques, but this also requires substantial infrastructure investment.

Another significant challenge is the potential for false positives, where legitimate network activities are misclassified as malicious. This can lead to unnecessary alerts and can overwhelm security teams. By leveraging unsupervised learning techniques, AI models can reduce the occurrence of false positives over time. These models can learn baseline behavior and detect genuine anomalies more accurately. Supervised learning can also be used in conjunction with expert feedback, refining the model's predictive accuracy.

Despite these challenges, the benefits of implementing AI-driven NIDS far outweigh the drawbacks. The ability to proactively monitor and defend a network is invaluable in mitigating the impact of cyber threats. Network-Based IDS act as an essential component in a multi-layered security strategy, providing a critical line of defense that works synergistically with other security measures, such as firewalls, endpoint protection, and manual threat hunting activities.

Furthermore, the role of AI in NIDS is expected to grow as technological advancements continue. Future iterations of NIDS will likely incorporate even more sophisticated AI techniques, such as reinforcement learning, to continually improve detection capabilities. These systems will not only identify threats but also automatically respond to mitigate them. Automated response mechanisms, driven by AI, can immediately quarantine compromised assets, block malicious traffic, and alert security teams to take further action.

In essence, Network-Based IDS are an indispensable element of modern cybersecurity strategies. They provide the necessary vigilance and analytical power to keep pace with the rapid evolution of cyber threats. As AI continues to evolve, so too will the capabilities of NIDS, ensuring that networks remain robustly defended against both known and emerging threats. The advent of AI in NIDS marks a significant leap forward in the realm of digital defense, offering unparalleled protection for critical infrastructure worldwide.

For cybersecurity professionals, the integration of AI into NIDS represents an exciting frontier. By staying updated with the latest advancements and actively incorporating these technologies into their defense strategies, organizations can significantly enhance their security posture. Whether it's through machine learning models that learn from traffic patterns or NLP algorithms that decode malicious communications, AI-driven NIDS will be a cornerstone of cybersecurity in the years to come.

Host-Based IDS - Host-Based Intrusion Detection Systems (HIDS) hold a pivotal role in modern cybersecurity architectures, especially as they are increasingly infused with AI capabilities. Unlike network-based IDS which monitors traffic across entire networks, HIDS are focused on individual endpoints. These systems operate by examining the internals of computing devices, such as desktops, servers, or even virtual machines, to identify signs of malicious activity.

HIDS provide a granular level of security by inspecting file integrity, system logs, running processes, and user behaviors specific to each host. Traditional HIDS relied heavily on signature-based detection mechanisms, which required databases of known threats that are continuously updated. However, the evolving landscape of cyber threats necessitates a more adaptive approach, and this is where AI steps in. AI-driven HIDS can analyze vast datasets, identify patterns indicative of novel threats, and adapt by learning from new data over time. Machine Learning (ML) algorithms, for instance, can evaluate sequences of system calls, flagging those which deviate from typical behavior as potential intrusions.

One of the primary benefits of AI-integrated HIDS is the ability to perform anomaly detection at a micro-level. By establishing behavioral baselines for each system user or application, AI algorithms can signal irregularities that may signify malicious intent. This level of detection is particularly advantageous for identifying zero-day exploits and advanced persistent threats (APTs) that are designed to evade traditional security measures. Through learning and adaptation, these AI systems continually refine what they consider 'normal,' thereby improving their detection capabilities.

Moreover, the deployment of AI-enhanced HIDS involves leveraging techniques like Natural Language Processing (NLP) to scrutinize log files and audit trails. NLP can process unstructured data, making sense of seemingly unrelated anomalies by correlating events that might go unnoticed with traditional heuristic methods. This capability is crucial for identifying patterns that indicate a compromise, such as unusual login times, atypical data access patterns, or unexpected modifications to system files.

AI doesn't just improve the accuracy of HIDS; it also enhances their efficiency. Manual review of intrusion alerts is both time-consuming and prone to human error. AI systems can significantly reduce the volume of false positives that security analysts must sift through, allowing them to focus on genuine threats. This streamlining of operations not only boosts productivity but also leads to faster incident response times. Real-time alerting mechanisms powered by AI ensure that suspicious activities are flagged instantaneously, allowing for immediate investigation and remediation.

It's also worth noting the integration of deep learning models in HIDS. Unlike traditional machine learning models that require feature engineering - a process of selecting and transforming variables used in predictive modeling - deep learning models autonomously extract features from raw data. This self-sufficiency ensures that the models evolve with every new dataset, becoming more sophisticated at spotting unauthorized activities. As cyber threats become more complex, the role of deep learning in HIDS will become even more critical.

Another aspect where AI excels is the contextual analysis of potential threats. HIDS equipped with AI can cross-reference anomalies against global threat databases and intelligence feeds, assessing the broader context before flagging an action as malicious. For example, a suspicious file execution might be cross-referenced with recent malware reports or threat intelligence data, providing a more comprehensive analysis that leads to more informed decision-making.

The implementation of AI in HIDS also introduces challenges that the industry must navigate. One such challenge is the risk of overreliance on AI models, which, if not properly trained and updated, can lead to security lapses. The dynamic nature of cyber threats requires continuous learning and adaptation, making the quality of data and the regular updating of models pivotal. Another challenge is the requirement for computational resources; AI, particularly deep learning, necessitates significant computational power and memory, which can be a limiting factor for some organizations.

Additionally, ethical considerations arise in the deployment of AI-driven HIDS. It's essential to ensure transparency in how these AI models make decisions, as opaque algorithms can lead to issues with accountability. Appropriate measures should be taken to maintain user privacy while amassing the data required for the effective operation of these systems. Implementing robust mechanisms for auditability and explainability of AI decisions is vital to address these ethical concerns.

Despite these challenges, the benefits of AI-enhanced HIDS are manifold. They can offer unparalleled intrusion detection capabilities, dramatically decreasing the window of vulnerability and enhancing overall system resilience. By combining the analytical power of AI with traditional cybersecurity measures, HIDS can offer a layered defense strategy, each layer tailored to thwarting different types of intrusions.

There's a growing trend toward hybrid environments, incorporating both on-premises and cloud infrastructures. AI-driven HIDS are particularly well-suited for these mixed environments. They can dynamically adapt to the varying security postures of different platforms, providing seamless protection across diverse infrastructures. This adaptability is essential as organizations increasingly adopt multi-cloud and hybrid-cloud architectures, where the complexity of managing security is significantly amplified.

Furthermore, AI in HIDS is not just a reactive measure anymore. With predictive analytics, these systems can forecast potential threats based on historical data and current trends. This predictive capability allows for proactive measures to be put in place before an actual intrusion happens, significantly bolstering an organization's security posture.

Looking to the future, the evolution of AI in HIDS will continue, driven by advancements in AI technologies and the ever-changing threat landscape. Quantum computing, enhanced AI algorithms, and more substantial data analytics capabilities promise to further revolutionize HIDS. Collaborative AI systems where multiple AI models work in concert, exchanging data and insights in real-time, could represent the next wave of cybersecurity innovation.

In conclusion, Host-Based Intrusion Detection Systems augmented with AI present a formidable defense against a myriad of cyber threats. They offer an advanced level of scrutiny that legacy systems cannot match, making them an indispensable asset in contemporary cybersecurity strategies. Equipped with machine learning, deep learning, and predictive analytics, these systems exemplify how AI is fundamentally transforming the digital defense landscape.

Chapter 5:
AI in Threat Prevention

In a constantly evolving cyber landscape, AI-driven threat prevention represents the cutting edge of proactive digital defense, stepping in before potential breaches can wreak havoc. AI empowers us with predictive analytics, allowing systems to anticipate and neutralize threats by identifying patterns that often elude human analysts. By leveraging machine learning algorithms, these systems can autonomously streamline the patch management process, ensuring vulnerabilities are mitigated swiftly and efficiently. With AI's capability to adapt and learn from new data, organizations are better positioned to fend off advanced attacks, turning potential crises into manageable events. In essence, AI transforms the reactive stance of traditional cybersecurity into a more dynamic and anticipatory model, creating a robust line of defense against an ever-growing array of cyber threats.

Proactive Defense Mechanisms

In the ever-evolving landscape of cybersecurity, the adage "prevention is better than cure" rings especially true. By leveraging AI, proactive defense mechanisms have emerged as indispensable tools in the fight against cyber threats. These mechanisms aim to preemptively identify and mitigate vulnerabilities before they can be exploited, effectively reducing the attack surface of a given system.

One of the key strategies in proactive defense is the deployment of AI-driven vulnerability scanners. Traditional vulnerability assessments can be labor-intensive and error-prone, often missing nuanced indicators of potential threats. AI enhances the speed and accuracy of these scans by employing techniques such as machine learning and natural language processing to analyze patterns and historical data. This enables the system to not only identify existing vulnerabilities but also predict emerging ones based on evolving threat landscapes.

Moreover, AI plays a pivotal role in threat intelligence gathering. By continuously scouring the web, dark web, and various data repositories, AI systems can aggregate and synthesize vast amounts of threat data in real-time. This intelligence is then used to inform security policies, update threat databases, and generate alerts about potential risks. AI's ability to process and interpret unstructured data sets it apart from traditional methods, making it possible to uncover more complex and stealthy threats.

Another cornerstone of proactive defense is predictive analytics. This facet of AI applies statistical models and machine learning algorithms to historical data in order to forecast future security incidents. Predictive analytics can determine the likelihood of specific types of attacks, enabling organizations to allocate their resources more effectively. For instance, if the model predicts an uptick in ransomware attacks during a particular period, companies can bolster their defenses accordingly, implementing stricter controls and educating employees about potential phishing attempts.

Artificial Intelligence also excels in the creation and management of dynamic honeypots—decoy systems intended to attract and monitor cyber attackers. Traditional honeypots often require considerable manual oversight to remain effective. AI mitigates this by autonomously configuring and updating honeypots in response to detected changes in the threat environment. When a honeypot is compromised, AI can analyze the attack vectors, providing valuable insights into the tactics, techniques, and procedures (TTPs) of cybercriminals. These insights are then fed back into the system to enhance future threat prevention measures.

Machine learning models are also central to implementing behavioral analysis for proactive defense. These models establish a baseline of normal activity by analyzing user and entity behavior over time. Any deviation from the established norm triggers an alert, allowing security teams to investigate potential threats before they escalate. Unlike conventional methods that rely on rigid rules and signatures, behavior-based detection is inherently adaptive, making it far more effective against sophisticated and previously unknown threats.

Another significant advantage of AI in proactive defense is its role in integration and automation. Security orchestration and automation response (SOAR) platforms leverage AI to unify various cybersecurity tools and processes. By automating routine tasks such as log analysis, threat hunting, and incident triage, SOAR systems free up valuable human resources for more strategic initiatives. This not only enhances operational efficiency but also ensures a quicker and more coordinated response to potential threats.

Additionally, AI has revolutionized patch management by making it more proactive and less reactive. Traditional patch management is often cumbersome and fraught with delays, leaving systems exposed to known vulnerabilities. AI-driven tools can automate the identification, testing, and deployment of patches, significantly reducing the window of vulnerability. These tools can prioritize patches based on the criticality of the threat and the specific configurations of the system, ensuring that the most pressing vulnerabilities are addressed first.

The transformation brought about by AI extends to endpoint protection as well. Modern endpoint protection platforms (EPP) equipped with AI capabilities offer real-time monitoring and automated threat containment. These systems analyze a plethora of data points from endpoints, identifying potential threats based on behavioral anomalies and known threat indicators. Upon detecting suspicious activity, AI can isolate the affected endpoint, preventing lateral movement and containing the threat before it can proliferate.

Moreover, AI enhances the effectiveness of spam filters and email security solutions, which are vital components of a proactive defense strategy. By employing natural language processing and advanced machine learning algorithms, these systems can detect phishing attempts that traditional filters might miss. They analyze email content, sender reputation, and even the behavioral traits of the recipient to discern whether an email is likely to be malicious. This significantly reduces the risk of phishing attacks, which are a common entry point for larger security breaches.

Proactive defense mechanisms also benefit from collaborative AI systems. These platforms enable organizations to share threat intelligence and security insights in real-time without compromising sensitive information. By pooling data and resources, a collective defense mechanism is established, which is far stronger than any isolated effort. AI facilitates this collaboration by standardizing and anonymizing the shared data, ensuring that it can be readily consumed and acted upon by all participants while maintaining privacy and compliance.

Furthermore, the convergence of AI and blockchain technologies promises to elevate proactive defense to new heights. Blockchain's immutable ledger provides a transparent and tamper-proof record of transactions, making it an ideal platform for logging security events and sharing threat intelligence. AI can analyze blockchain data to identify patterns and anomalies that signify potential threats. This synergy enhances the trustworthiness and integrity of threat intelligence, providing a robust foundation for anticipatory action.

Of course, no defense mechanism is infallible, and proactive defense is no exception. AI systems must be continually updated and trained on new data to remain effective. This requires a concerted effort to ensure that AI models are not only accurate but also free from biases that could be exploited by adversaries. Regular audits and the incorporation of ethical AI practices are essential to maintaining the efficacy and fairness of these systems.

In conclusion, AI has fundamentally transformed proactive defense mechanisms in cybersecurity. Its capabilities in vulnerability assessment, threat intelligence, predictive analytics, and automation have made it an indispensable asset for any comprehensive security strategy. By preemptively identifying and mitigating potential threats, AI not only protects critical assets but also fosters a more resilient and adaptive security posture. As the cyber threat landscape continues to evolve, the role of AI in proactive defense will undoubtedly become even more crucial, paving the way for a safer digital future.

Predictive Analytics

In the rapidly evolving landscape of cybersecurity, the ability to foresee and act on potential threats before they materialize is invaluable. Predictive analytics plays a crucial role in AI-driven threat prevention. By harnessing vast amounts of data, predictive analytics can identify trends, predict future outcomes, and provide actionable insights that bolster a proactive defense strategy.

At its core, predictive analytics involves using historical data to make informed predictions about future events. In the context of threat prevention, this entails analyzing patterns and trends in cyber attack data to anticipate potential threats. Techniques such as machine learning, statistical modeling, and data mining are employed to uncover these hidden patterns. Once identified, these patterns guide the development of models that can predict future cyber attacks. These predictive models are continuously refined as they ingest more data, improving their accuracy over time.

The predictive models rely heavily on machine learning algorithms. These algorithms scrutinize historical data to detect anomalies and identify patterns indicative of malicious activity. For instance, if a particular type of malware tends to target specific vulnerabilities in a system, predictive analytics can flag these vulnerabilities before an attack occurs. This enables security teams to patch vulnerabilities preemptively, significantly reducing the risk of compromise.

Another key component of predictive analytics is data integration. Cybersecurity ecosystems are vast and intricate, comprising diverse data sources ranging from server logs and network traffic data to user behaviors and threat intelligence feeds. Integrating these disparate data sources is crucial for developing a comprehensive threat landscape. Predictive analytics tools aggregate and analyze data from these varied sources, providing a holistic view of the threat environment and enabling more accurate predictions.

One of the most compelling applications of predictive analytics in threat prevention is the identification of zero-day vulnerabilities. Unlike known vulnerabilities, zero-day vulnerabilities are unknown to the security community and can be exploited by attackers without warning. Predictive analytics enhances the capability to detect behavioral patterns and system anomalies that may indicate the presence of a zero-day vulnerability. Proactively addressing these vulnerabilities minimizes the potential damage caused by such attacks.

Moreover, predictive analytics isn't just about identifying and mitigating threats; it's also about prioritizing them. In an environment flooded with potential alerts, distinguishing critical threats from low-priority ones is paramount. Predictive analytics helps prioritize threats based on criteria such as the potential impact on the organization's assets, the likelihood of exploitation, and historical attack data. This prioritization ensures that security resources are focused where they are most needed, optimizing the defensive posture of the organization.

However, the implementation of predictive analytics in threat prevention is not without challenges. Foremost among these is the issue of data quality. Predictive models are only as good as the data they're trained on. Inconsistent, incomplete, or biased data can adversely affect the accuracy of predictions. Ensuring high-quality, relevant data is paramount for effective predictive analytics.

Another challenge lies in the dynamic nature of cyber threats. Attackers continually evolve their techniques to bypass traditional security measures. To stay ahead, predictive analytics models must be adaptive, continually learning from new data and adjusting their predictions accordingly. This requires a robust infrastructure capable of handling real-time data processing and model updating.

Despite these challenges, the benefits of integrating predictive analytics into threat prevention strategies are immense. Organizations that leverage predictive analytics can transition from a reactive to a proactive security stance, anticipating and mitigating threats before they can cause harm. This shift not only enhances the organization's security posture but also reduces response times and mitigates the impact of potential breaches.

Additionally, the interpretability of predictive models is an area of active research and development. Understanding how and why a model makes specific predictions is crucial for trusting and acting upon its insights. Techniques such as model explainability and interpretability frameworks are being developed to provide transparency into the decision-making process of predictive models. This transparency helps security analysts comprehend the rationale behind predictions, facilitating informed decision-making and fostering trust in the analytical process.

Predictive analytics also plays a pivotal role in threat intelligence sharing. By pooling data from multiple organizations, collaborative predictive models can be developed, offering a broader view of the threat landscape. These models can detect patterns and trends that may not be visible in a single organization's data alone, enhancing the overall efficacy of threat prevention efforts across the industry.

Moreover, as artificial intelligence and machine learning technologies continue to advance, the accuracy and capabilities of predictive analytics will only improve. Future developments may see the integration of advanced techniques such as deep learning and natural language processing, further refining the predictive capabilities of cybersecurity systems.

In conclusion, the integration of predictive analytics into AI-driven threat prevention represents a significant advancement in the field of cybersecurity. By leveraging historical data, machine learning algorithms, and advanced data integration techniques, predictive analytics can anticipate and mitigate potential threats, transforming the traditional reactive approach to cybersecurity into a proactive and robust defense strategy.

As organizations continue to face an ever-growing array of cyber threats, the importance of predictive analytics in maintaining a secure digital environment cannot be overstated. By investing in and embracing these technologies, organizations can stay one step ahead of cyber attackers, safeguarding their assets and ensuring the integrity of their digital infrastructure.

Automated Patch Management

When discussing AI in threat prevention, one of the standout applications is automated patch management. Traditionally, patch management has been a labor-intensive process, often resulting in delays that leave systems vulnerable to exploits. With the integration of AI, however, the landscape has changed dramatically.

At its core, patch management involves identifying, testing, and installing patches or updates to software applications and systems. These patches can fix vulnerabilities, correct bugs, or improve performance. The challenge historically has been the time lag between patch release and implementation. During this window, systems remain exposed to known vulnerabilities. Automated patch management systems powered by AI tackle this issue head-on by minimizing human intervention and significantly reducing the time needed to patch vulnerabilities.

AI-driven patch management systems can autonomously monitor various software platforms for emerging patches. Using natural language processing (NLP), these systems scan through release notes, update bulletins, and even forums to detect new patches or vulnerabilities. This proactive approach ensures that patches are identified as soon as they are publicized, thereby mitigating the window of vulnerability.

But identifying patches is only a part of the solution. Where AI excels is in the next steps: assessing the relevance of these patches to the specific configuration and environment of the organization, and then strategically planning their deployment. Machine learning models, trained on historical data, can predict the potential impact of a patch on the system's performance, ensuring that critical updates are prioritized without compromising stability.

Moreover, AI can automate the testing phase. One of the significant barriers to fast patch deployment is the need to test patches in a controlled environment to ensure they don't break existing applications. Using AI, these tests can be carried out in virtualized environments that mirror the production setup. If the patch passes these automated tests, the system can proceed to deploy it across the network.

Deployment strategies further benefit from AI's predictive analytics capabilities. For instance, AI can analyze network traffic patterns and user behavior to determine the optimal times for deploying patches, ensuring minimal disruption to business operations. If a potential conflict or issue is detected during deployment, AI can also roll back changes and alert human administrators for further action.

The integration of AI in patch management also brings enhanced tracking and reporting functionalities. Advanced systems can generate detailed reports on patch status, compliance levels, and even predict future patching needs based on emerging threat landscapes. These insights are invaluable for cybersecurity professionals, allowing for more efficient resource allocation and strategic planning.

In essence, automated patch management isn't just about speed; it's about intelligence. By leveraging AI, organizations can ensure that their systems are not only up-to-date but also secure against known and emerging threats. This intelligent approach to patch management is a testament to how AI can transform traditionally reactive cybersecurity processes into proactive defense mechanisms.

Moreover, automated patch management contributes significantly to organizational compliance. Many regulatory frameworks, such as GDPR and HIPAA, mandate timely patching of security vulnerabilities. AI-driven systems can ensure continuous compliance by maintaining an up-to-date inventory of patches and their deployment status. This reduces the risk of penalties and enhances the organization's overall security posture.

While the benefits of automated patch management are substantial, it's essential to recognize that it isn't a silver bullet. Organizations need to complement it with other AI-driven cybersecurity measures to create a comprehensive defense strategy. Automated patch management effectively addresses the vulnerabilities related to known threats, but it needs to work in conjunction with real-time threat detection and incident response systems to tackle zero-day exploits and sophisticated attacks.

Security teams should also invest in ongoing training and development. While AI handles the bulk of patch management tasks, human oversight remains crucial. Cybersecurity professionals need to understand how these AI systems operate and be prepared to intervene when necessary. This dual approach ensures robustness and reliability in patch management processes.

Automated patch management is a clear example of how AI is revolutionizing cybersecurity. By marrying speed with intelligence, AI-driven systems provide robust, timely, and efficient solutions to patch vulnerabilities. This not only enhances an organization's security stance but also ensures compliance and operational continuity. As AI continues to evolve, we can expect even more sophisticated and integrated approaches to automated patch management, paving the way for a more secure digital future.

Chapter 6:
AI in Incident Response

When it comes to incident response, the integration of Artificial Intelligence (AI) is nothing short of transformative. Traditional methods of handling security incidents often involved manual processes that could be time-consuming and prone to human error. Now, AI-driven solutions expedite the entire process, from detection to resolution. Automated Incident Response Systems can ascertain the scope and impact of an attack within moments, offering real-time insights that bolster decision-making. Complementing these systems, AI-driven forensics tools sift through vast amounts of data to identify and analyze malicious activities with pinpoint accuracy, thereby significantly reducing the time needed to understand and mitigate threats. Furthermore, AI enhances crisis management by orchestrating coordinated responses across various security protocols, ensuring that the right actions are taken at the right time. This multi-faceted approach not only minimizes damage but also boosts the resiliency and agility of organizations in fending off and recovering from cyber attacks.

Automated Incident Response Systems

As the complexity and frequency of cyber threats continue to escalate, the need for rapid and efficient incident response becomes critical. Automated Incident Response Systems (AIRS) leverage the power of Artificial Intelligence to address this necessity, transforming the way cybersecurity professionals combat threats. By reducing human intervention, these systems can respond to incidents in real-time, minimizing potential damage and downtime.

One of the primary benefits of AIRS is speed. Traditional incident response requires manual analysis and decision-making, often resulting in delayed reactions. In contrast, AI-driven systems can analyze data, identify threats, and execute predefined response protocols within seconds. This rapid response is crucial in containing threats before they can proliferate across networks and compromise sensitive data.

Moreover, the accuracy of AIRS cannot be understated. These systems utilize machine learning algorithms to continuously learn from past incidents and adapt to evolving threats. This adaptive learning process ensures that the system becomes more effective over time, improving its ability to detect and respond to new types of cyber-attacks.

Integrating an Automated Incident Response System into an organization's cybersecurity architecture often involves several core components. First, real-time monitoring tools are essential to continuously gather and analyze data across the network. These tools provide the raw input that the AIRS needs to function effectively.

Next, the core AI engine processes this data, leveraging pattern recognition and anomaly detection techniques. This engine identifies potential threats and correlates them with known attack patterns. Once a threat is identified, the system's response module activates, executing predefined mitigation measures. These measures might include isolating affected systems, blocking malicious IP addresses, or deploying patches to vulnerable software.

One significant advantage of AIRS is the ability to handle multiple incidents simultaneously. While human analysts can be overwhelmed during a large-scale attack, automated systems can manage numerous threats at once without fatigue or error. This parallel processing capability is particularly valuable in defending against complex, multi-vector attacks.

The integration of AIRS also enhances an organization's compliance posture. Many regulatory frameworks, such as GDPR and HIPAA, require swift responses to data breaches and cybersecurity incidents. An AI-driven system can help organizations meet these regulatory demands by ensuring incidents are detected and addressed promptly, thereby reducing the risk of non-compliance penalties.

However, the effectiveness of AIRS is not without challenges. Implementing such systems requires significant upfront investment in both technology and talent. Ensuring that the AI models are trained on comprehensive and representative data sets is critical. Without proper training data, the system's performance can be suboptimal, potentially overlooking threats or generating false positives.

Additionally, there is the challenge of integrating AIRS with existing cybersecurity tools and protocols. These systems need to work harmoniously with traditional firewalls, intrusion detection systems, and endpoint security solutions. Seamless integration ensures that the AIRS can leverage the full spectrum of an organization's cybersecurity infrastructure.

Human oversight remains a crucial component of effective incident response, even with advanced AIRS in place. Cybersecurity experts must continuously review and refine the automated response protocols and investigate incidents that the AI system can't resolve. This ongoing collaboration between humans and machines creates a robust defense mechanism that leverages the strengths of both.

Advanced reporting and audit trails are another vital feature of AIRS. Comprehensive logging of incident responses allows organizations to perform post-incident analysis, identifying weaknesses and areas for improvement. These logs also provide valuable insights during regulatory audits and help in refining AI models for future incidents.

To further enhance the efficacy of AIRS, many organizations are adopting a hybrid model that combines automated systems with human analysts. This approach ensures that while AI handles routine incidents, more complex threats receive the attention of seasoned cybersecurity professionals. This synergy between automation and human expertise creates a more resilient and adaptive incident response framework.

Looking forward, the evolution of AIRS will be closely tied to advancements in AI and machine learning. As these technologies continue to evolve, we can expect even more sophisticated response mechanisms capable of anticipating and neutralizing threats before they materialize. Continuous improvement in AI-driven analytics and anomaly detection will further enhance the precision and reliability of these systems.

In conclusion, Automated Incident Response Systems represent a significant leap forward in the realm of cybersecurity. By harnessing the power of AI, these systems offer unparalleled speed, accuracy, and scalability in responding to cyber threats. While challenges in implementation and integration exist, the benefits far outweigh the drawbacks. As cyber threats continue to evolve, the role of AIRS will become increasingly indispensable, providing organizations with the robust defenses needed to protect their digital assets.

The future of incident response lies in the strategic blend of artificial intelligence and human expertise, creating a dynamic and adaptive security posture capable of meeting the challenges of an ever-changing cyber landscape.

AI-Driven Forensics

As the landscape of cyber threats grows more complex, so does the need for robust tools to investigate security breaches. AI-driven forensics represents the cutting edge in incident response, transforming how cybersecurity professionals approach digital investigations. In essence, this technology leverages artificial intelligence to enhance the detection, analysis, and remediation of cyber incidents, offering capabilities that traditional methods simply can't match.

One of the foremost advantages of AI-driven forensics is its ability to sift through massive quantities of data at unprecedented speeds. When a breach occurs, time is of the essence, and the longer it takes to analyze the data, the higher the potential damage. Traditional forensics methods, which often involve manual examination, can be both time-consuming and prone to human error. AI, however, can automate and expedite these processes, offering real-time insights and enabling quicker response times.

Imagine trying to find a specific needle in a world-sized haystack. That's often what manual forensics feels like. AI algorithms, particularly those utilizing machine learning and deep learning, can rapidly identify patterns and anomalies indicative of malicious activity. By comparing current data points with historical data, these algorithms can spot deviations that might escape the notice of human analysts.

Moreover, AI-driven forensics doesn't just identify what happened; it helps determine how and why it happened. Utilizing advanced techniques such as natural language processing (NLP), AI can analyze logs, communications, and other textual data to uncover the tactics, techniques, and procedures (TTPs) used by threat actors. This level of insight aids in recreating the timeline of an attack, providing invaluable context for understanding the breach.

Behavior analysis is another crucial component of AI-driven forensics. While traditional methods might focus on static indicators of compromise (IoCs), AI systems assess behavioral patterns over time. For instance, an employee suddenly accessing large volumes of sensitive data during odd hours might trigger an alert. Such nuanced detection, facilitated by machine learning models, augments the thoroughness of the investigation.

And then there's the matter of integration. AI-driven forensics tools can seamlessly integrate with existing security infrastructures, complementing other security measures like intrusion detection systems (IDS) and automated incident response platforms. This holistic approach ensures that data collected from various sources is analyzed cohesively, providing a comprehensive view of the incident.

Crucially, AI's role isn't just limited to post-incident analysis. Predictive forensics, an emerging field, leverages AI to anticipate potential attack scenarios before they materialize fully. By simulating different breach scenarios based on existing vulnerabilities and known threat vectors, organizations can proactively fortify their defenses and even pre-empt attacks.

Of course, the efficacy of AI in forensics depends largely on the quality and quantity of data it has access to. That's where big data analytics comes into play. AI-driven forensics systems consume vast amounts of data from diverse sources—network logs, endpoint data, threat intelligence feeds, and even social media chatter. Machine learning models then process this data to extract actionable intelligence, guiding the forensic investigation.

Collaborative AI is also making strides in the realm of digital forensics. In scenarios where insights from various AI systems are pooled together, the collective intelligence can be significantly more powerful. For example, federated learning systems allow different organizations to share insights gleaned from their respective datasets without exposing sensitive information, thereby enriching the AI algorithms' ability to detect and analyze threats.

This brings us to the future potential of AI-driven forensics. As AI technologies continue to evolve, we can anticipate even more sophisticated capabilities. Consider, for instance, the integration of AI with augmented reality (AR) for forensic investigation. In such a setup, investigators could utilize AR headsets to visualize data flows and attack vectors in real-time, overlaying critical insights directly onto their physical environment.

The use of blockchain technology in AI-driven forensics is another area worth mentioning. Blockchain can ensure the immutability and integrity of forensic evidence, providing a tamper-proof ledger of all actions taken during an investigation. This can be particularly valuable for legal proceedings, where the chain of custody and the integrity of evidence are paramount.

Nevertheless, the advent of AI-driven forensics doesn't come without challenges. One noteworthy concern is the potential for AI systems to be fooled by adversarial tactics. Complex algorithms, especially those relying on deep learning, can sometimes be misled by carefully crafted adversarial inputs. As such, continuous updates and rigorous testing of AI models are essential to maintain their reliability and integrity.

Ethical considerations can't be ignored either. While AI enhances the efficiency and accuracy of forensic investigations, it also raises questions about privacy and bias. It's crucial to ensure that AI algorithms are transparent and that their decision-making processes are explainable. Furthermore, steps must be taken to mitigate any biases inherent in the training data to prevent skewed analysis outcomes.

Another significant challenge lies in the integration of AI-driven tools with existing forensic workflows. Many organizations may find it daunting to transition from traditional methods to AI-enhanced processes. Therefore, training and upskilling cybersecurity professionals to work effectively with AI tools is imperative. Besides, robust frameworks and guidelines must be established to govern the use of AI in forensic investigations, ensuring consistency and reliability.

Despite these challenges, the benefits of AI-driven forensics are too significant to overlook. As cyber threats become more sophisticated, the marriage of artificial intelligence and digital forensics promises to be a game-changer. It equips cybersecurity professionals with the advanced tools needed to stay ahead of adversaries, ensuring quicker, more accurate, and comprehensive investigations.

In conclusion, AI-driven forensics marks a pivotal evolution in the field of incident response. By dramatically improving the speed and accuracy of forensic analysis, AI provides a formidable weapon against the ever-evolving landscape of cyber threats. As technologies advance, so too will the capabilities of AI-driven forensics, continually pushing the boundaries of what's possible in digital defense.

Crisis Management

When a cybersecurity breach occurs, it's not just about containing the immediate damage—it's about managing the entire crisis scenario with precision and foresight. AI is proving to be a formidable ally in this area, revolutionizing how we approach crisis management from the ground up. One core strength of AI lies in its ability to rapidly analyze vast amounts of data and identify threats in real-time, which is critical for effective crisis management.

In the initial moments of a cyber crisis, the speed and accuracy of response are crucial. AI-driven systems can immediately start working on containment by isolating affected segments of a network. Real-time monitoring systems powered by AI can detect irregular activities that signify a breach, allowing for swift action. These systems can place compromised accounts on lockdown, terminate malicious processes, or block harmful traffic within seconds. Speed is of the essence, and AI's rapid response capabilities offer organizations a crucial head start.

Beyond immediate containment, AI plays a central role in the forensic investigation that follows a cybersecurity incident. AI-driven forensics tools can sift through terabytes of logs, network flows, and other data sources to piece together the sequence of events that led to the breach. This investigative phase provides vital insights into the nature of the attack vectors employed and the vulnerabilities exploited. Understanding these elements is critical to not only mitigate the current crisis but also to bolster defenses against future threats.

AI can also aid in managing public relations during a cyber crisis. Natural Language Processing (NLP) algorithms can analyze social media chatter and news articles to gauge public sentiment about the incident. This real-time sentiment analysis allows organizations to tailor their communication strategies, ensuring timely and effective messaging. Well-crafted messages can help maintain customer trust and mitigate reputational damage.

Additionally, AI can streamline coordination among internal teams and external stakeholders. Automated communication platforms can keep all parties informed about the current status of the crisis, steps being taken to manage it, and what might be required from them. These platforms ensure that everyone remains on the same page, reducing confusion and delays that could exacerbate the crisis.

In more advanced scenarios, AI can simulate various crisis scenarios to prepare organizations in advance. These simulations can include different types of cyber attacks, operational disruptions, and even insider threats. By running these simulations, organizations can identify potential weaknesses in their crisis response plans and make necessary adjustments. The ability to anticipate and prepare for various crisis scenarios means that when a real incident occurs, the response can be more efficient and effective. AI can also provide predictive insights, which is crucial for proactive crisis management. Analyzing historical data and recognizing patterns allows AI to forecast potential future incidents. This predictive capability can help organizations anticipate and mitigate risks before they materialize, adding a preventive layer to crisis management strategies.

Another critical role of AI in crisis management is in post-incident analysis. After the threat has been neutralized, AI systems can generate comprehensive reports detailing what happened, how it was handled, and what could be done better next time. These reports can be invaluable not only for internal review but also for regulatory compliance. Understanding the full scope of an incident and the effectiveness of the response provides learning opportunities that can shape future crisis management policies and procedures.

AI encourages a mentality shift from reactive to proactive crisis management. Instead of merely responding to a crisis after it happens, AI-equipped systems enable organizations to anticipate potential crises and prepare for various scenarios. This forward-looking approach can drastically reduce the impact of any incident, not only in terms of immediate damage control but also by mitigating long-term repercussions.

Integrating AI into crisis management also necessitates a harmonious relationship between human expertise and automated systems. While AI can handle data processing and threat containment with unmatched speed, human oversight remains crucial for nuanced decision-making and ethical considerations. This collaboration ensures that while AI manages the brunt of the technical load, human experts can focus on strategic planning and ethical ramifications, further enhancing the overall crisis management framework.

As organizations embrace AI for crisis management, continuous learning becomes essential. AI systems are only as good as the data they are trained on and the algorithms that drive them. Therefore, regular updates and ongoing training protocols are vital to keeping AI-driven crisis management systems at the cutting edge. This continuous learning loop allows AI to adapt to emerging threats and evolving crisis management best practices, ensuring that organizations remain resilient and prepared.

Incorporating AI into the crisis management framework brings several advantages, but it also introduces new challenges. Ensuring data integrity, managing false positives, and navigating the ethical implications of automated decision-making are some of the complexities that come with AI integration. Therefore, a balanced approach that leverages the strengths of both AI and human expertise is critical for achieving optimal crisis management outcomes. The ultimate goal is a seamless and efficient response to cyber incidents that mitigates damage and builds resilience against future threats.

In summary, AI's role in crisis management is transformative, offering unprecedented capabilities for real-time threat detection, rapid response, and comprehensive post-incident analysis. While challenges exist, the advantages far outweigh them, making AI an indispensable tool in the modern cybersecurity arsenal. By embracing AI, organizations not only enhance their crisis management capabilities but also position themselves to better navigate the evolving landscape of cyber threats, ensuring a more secure and resilient future.

Chapter 7:
Leveraging Big Data

In the rapidly evolving domain of cybersecurity, leveraging big data has become an indispensable strategy. With the sheer volume, variety, and velocity of data generated every second, it's vital for organizations to harness this information to bolster their cyber defenses. Big data allows for the collection and analysis of extensive datasets, providing critical insights into potential threats and vulnerabilities. By applying advanced analytics and machine learning algorithms to this data, cybersecurity professionals can identify patterns and anomalies that could indicate malicious activity. However, big data in cybersecurity is not without its challenges, such as ensuring data quality, managing vast amounts of information, and addressing privacy concerns. Mastering these aspects enables more robust threat detection, prevention, and response, ultimately fortifying a system's overall security posture.

The Role of Big Data in Cyber Defense

When delving into how artificial intelligence (AI) transforms cybersecurity, an essential element is understanding the role that big data plays. In the realm of cyber defense, the complexity and volume of data generated can be overwhelming. Every interaction, transaction, or digital communication generates a data point, and the accumulation of these data points forms big data. Cybersecurity professionals are leveraging this massive repository of information to identify, assess, and mitigate threats more effectively than ever before.

The first crucial aspect of big data in cyber defense is its capacity to offer deep insights through comprehensive data analysis. By aggregating data from multiple sources—such as network logs, user activity, and threat feeds—cyber defenders can construct a holistic view of the security landscape. This continuous data influx helps AI systems spot abnormal behavior and irregular patterns that could signify potential threats. In essence, big data acts as the eyes and ears of AI-driven cybersecurity solutions, furnishing the raw material from which actionable intelligence is derived.

Machine learning (ML) algorithms thrive on data, and big data provides an abundance of it. More data means better training for AI systems, which translates to more accurate threat detection and predictive capabilities. These algorithms can sift through petabytes of data, making sense of anomalies that humans might overlook. For example, an AI system might recognize a subtle shift in network traffic indicative of a low-and-slow attack designed to avoid detection. Without big data, training these systems on such nuanced deviations would be practically impossible.

Moreover, big data enables real-time threat detection and response. The volume and velocity of data generation mean that cyber threats can evolve quickly. Security Information and Event Management (SIEM) systems integrated with big data analytics can process billions of events per day, flagging any deviations from normal activity as a potential risk. In doing so, organizations can shift from a reactive to a proactive security posture, neutralizing threats before they can cause significant damage.

Big data also paves the way for more sophisticated threat intelligence. By analyzing data from diverse sources, such as dark web monitoring, open-source intelligence, and private threat feeds, cybersecurity teams can enrich their understanding of emerging threats. This enriched threat intelligence allows for robust threat modeling, where defenders can anticipate and mitigate risks based on historical and predictive analyses. The interplay between big data and AI can produce threat intelligence that's not only timely but also highly contextual, enabling more informed decision-making.

Data diversity is another critical aspect. The more varied the data, the more robust the learning and the better the AI systems can generalize from their training. Multiple data types—files, images, metadata, or log files—when analyzed together, can reveal hidden correlations and trends. For example, combining user behavior analytics (UBA) with endpoint data might uncover a potential insider threat that isolated analyses would miss. The diversity in data, therefore, becomes a strength, enhancing the accuracy and reliability of threat detection and response mechanisms.

Importantly, big data also informs the development of predictive analytics in cybersecurity. Predictive models, bolstered by extensive datasets, can forecast potential vulnerabilities and attacks before they occur. For instance, predictive analytics can scrutinize historical attack data to identify patterns that suggest the resurgence of a particular threat vector. By anticipating such trends, organizations can fortify their defenses in advance, creating a significant edge in threat prevention.

However, utilizing big data in cyber defense is not without its challenges. One such challenge is the sheer size of the data sets involved. Managing and processing large volumes of data requires substantial computational power and storage resources. It also requires skilled personnel who can interpret and analyze this data effectively. While AI can automate many processes, human oversight remains crucial to ensure accurate and contextually appropriate responses.

Another challenge is data quality. Inaccurate, incomplete, or outdated data can lead to false positives or, worse, missed threats. As the adage goes, "garbage in, garbage out." Ensuring data quality involves not just collecting the right data but also cleaning and processing it in ways that enhance its utility for AI-driven analyses. This may include normalizing data formats, removing duplicates, and validating source accuracy.

Scalability is a significant concern as well. As organizations grow, so does their data. Effective cybersecurity solutions must scale alongside this growth without compromising performance. This scalability involves both horizontal scaling, where resources are added to handle more data, and vertical scaling, where existing systems are enhanced to process data more efficiently. Technologies like cloud computing and distributed databases play a pivotal role in achieving this scalability, but these solutions come with their own set of security considerations that must be addressed.

Data privacy is another critical issue. Cybersecurity efforts must comply with regulations such as GDPR, HIPAA, and CCPA, which mandate rigorous standards for data protection and privacy. Leveraging big data while ensuring compliance requires a delicate balance. Organizations must implement robust data governance frameworks that include encryption, anonymization, and secure access controls to safeguard sensitive information while still deriving actionable intelligence from it.

The integration of big data tools with existing cybersecurity frameworks is also essential. Seamless integration ensures that data flows efficiently between different systems, enabling more effective threat detection and response. Open standards and APIs can facilitate this integration, allowing various tools and platforms to work together harmoniously. This interconnectedness enhances the overall security posture by enabling comprehensive and coordinated defense mechanisms.

Furthermore, the role of big data extends beyond threat detection and response to include post-incident analysis. After a security breach, big data analytics can aid in forensic investigations by providing a detailed audit trail of events leading up to the incident. This helps organizations understand the attack vector, identify vulnerabilities, and implement corrective measures to prevent future occurrences. In essence, big data not only helps in thwarting attacks but also in learning from them.

With the advent of AI and machine learning, the cybersecurity landscape has been irrevocably altered. Big data stands at the core of this transformation, providing the foundational layer upon which AI technologies operate. It enables faster, more accurate threat detection, enhances predictive capabilities, and offers deeper insights into potential vulnerabilities. However, the effective use of big data in cyber defense requires careful planning and execution, addressing challenges related to data volume, quality, scalability, and privacy.

As we continue to delve into the future of cybersecurity, the symbiotic relationship between big data and AI will only grow stronger. Cyber defenders will increasingly rely on big data not just for immediate threat mitigation, but for building resilient, adaptive, and intelligent security systems capable of evolving alongside emerging threats. Embracing this dynamic duo—big data and AI—will be key to staying ahead in the ever-changing cyber threat landscape.

The next section will explore data collection and analysis, delving deeper into how organizations can harness the power of big data for more robust and responsive cybersecurity measures. But as we've seen, without big data, the promise of AI in cyber defense would remain largely unfulfilled. Therefore, mastering the intricacies of big data is not just an option but a necessity for any organization serious about protecting its digital assets.

Data Collection and Analysis

Leveraging big data for cybersecurity involves intricate processes of data collection and analysis. These tasks are fundamental in maintaining robust digital defenses, providing the foundation upon which AI systems can effectively function. The sheer volume and variety of data required to safeguard systems from cyber threats make big data indispensable in modern cybersecurity strategies. As data continues to proliferate, so too does the potential to harness it for improved defense mechanisms.

Data collection in cybersecurity takes in information from numerous sources, including network traffic logs, endpoint devices, application logs, and even social media feeds. This diversity provides a broad perspective on the potential threats facing an organization. Consider the case of network traffic logs. Collecting data continuously from these logs enables AI systems to monitor activities and detect anomalies that could indicate a security breach.

Endpoint devices, such as computers and mobile phones, generate significant amounts of data that are essential for detecting threats. Each interaction, login attempt, and file access is logged, creating a digital trail that AI systems analyze to identify unauthorized activities. This type of granular data is crucial for mitigating threats at the user level, preventing breaches before they can escalate.

Another important aspect of data collection is harnessing data from application logs. Applications, especially those that are business-critical, are frequent targets of cyber-attacks. By collecting detailed logs from these applications, AI systems can detect unusual patterns indicative of an intrusion or malware activity. Application logs provide a view into the specific operations and processes that take place within software environments, making them a rich source of actionable intelligence.

Social media feeds have also emerged as a valuable data source for cybersecurity. Hackers often use social media for reconnaissance, phishing attacks, and spreading misinformation. By monitoring these feeds, AI algorithms can identify malicious activities and thwart potential attacks. This real-time data collection taps into the broader cyber threat landscape, giving organizations the intelligence they need to defend against sophisticated threats.

Once the data is collected, it must be prepared for analysis. This involves cleaning, processing, and ensuring the data's integrity. Data cleaning is crucial because noisy or irrelevant data can lead to inaccurate analysis, diluting the effectiveness of AI systems. This task involves removing duplicates, correcting errors, and standardizing formats to ensure consistency.

Next comes processing the data, where normalization techniques are employed to ensure different data formats can be analyzed together. Data transformation steps might also include converting raw data into a structured format, making it more suitable for AI algorithms. Processing is necessary to facilitate the smooth flow of information through different analytical stages, enabling the extraction of relevant insights.

The integrity of the data also plays a pivotal role in the accuracy of analysis. Ensuring that the data is unaltered and originates from reputable sources strengthens the reliability of the AI's findings. This can be achieved through cryptographic methods and validating data sources to safeguard against tampered information.

Following data preparation, we proceed to analysis. AI techniques like machine learning and deep learning require vast amounts of data for training and validation. In cybersecurity contexts, these techniques typically focus on identifying patterns and anomalies within the collected data. Machine learning models, for example, are trained on historical data to recognize the characteristics of known threats. Once trained, these models can predict and identify similar threats in real-time.

Deep learning models take this a step further, using advanced neural networks to detect subtle and complex patterns that might be missed by simpler algorithms. These models can analyze vast amounts of data at incredible speeds, making them ideal for real-time threat detection. They are particularly effective in identifying zero-day exploits and other advanced threats that do not follow known patterns.

Natural Language Processing (NLP) is another potent tool in the arsenal of AI for cybersecurity. NLP techniques analyze textual data, including code, configuration files, and even hacker communications. By understanding the context and semantics of this data, NLP models can identify suspicious activities and prevent attacks before they materialize.

Behavioral analysis is another key component of data analysis in cybersecurity. This approach focuses on monitoring and understanding the behavior of users and systems. By establishing baseline behaviors, AI systems can detect deviations that may indicate malicious activities. For instance, if a user's login patterns suddenly change or a system starts accessing data at unusual times, these anomalies can trigger alerts for further investigation.

In conclusion, data collection and analysis form the backbone of leveraging big data in cybersecurity. By harvesting vast amounts of data from diverse sources, cleaning and processing it, and analyzing it using advanced AI techniques, organizations can significantly enhance their cyber defenses. These processes provide the actionable intelligence needed to detect, prevent, and respond to threats in real-time. As cyber threats continue to evolve, the ability to effectively collect and analyze data will remain a critical factor in maintaining robust digital security.

Challenges of Big Data in Cybersecurity

Big data has revolutionized many fields, including cybersecurity. However, the integration of big data into cybersecurity is fraught with challenges that need addressing if we're to harness its full potential effectively. One of the significant hurdles revolves around the massive volume of data generated daily. Collecting, storing, processing, and analyzing this vast amount of data is an ongoing challenge, particularly when everything must happen in real-time.

The sheer volume of data also increases the complexity of threat detection. Cybercriminals exploit this complexity by planting subtle anomalies within mountains of data, hoping they go unnoticed amidst the noise. Traditional methods of filtering and analyzing data often fall short, making it difficult to distinguish between benign irregularities and actual threats. Identifying patterns indicative of cyber-attacks requires advanced algorithms and considerable computing power.

Furthermore, big data in cybersecurity necessitates highly skilled professionals. The integration of big data analytics in cyber defense demands expertise in both data science and cybersecurity. Unfortunately, there's a glaring skills gap in the current workforce. Bridging this gap requires substantial investment in training and development programs, which organizations may be reluctant to undertake due to cost constraints.

Speed is another vital factor. To fend off cyber threats, threat detection needs to be as close to real-time as possible. Big data analytics processes can be time-consuming, often resulting in delayed responses. These delays can give adversaries just enough time to exploit vulnerabilities, leading to potentially catastrophic breaches. Enhancing processing speed without compromising accuracy remains a significant challenge.

Data variety adds another layer of complexity. Cybersecurity data come from various sources, such as network logs, emails, social media, and more. Each type presents unique characteristics and requires different processing techniques. Standardizing and correlating these diverse data types to have a coherent and comprehensive view of the threat landscape is a daunting task.

Organizations also face challenges in ensuring the quality and accuracy of data. Poor data quality can lead to false positives and negatives in threat detection, hampering effective cybersecurity strategies. Ensuring high data quality demands rigorous validation and cleansing processes, which can be labor-intensive and time-consuming. Inaccurate data not only misguides security measures but also wastes valuable resources.

While managing big data, privacy concerns are paramount. Collecting and analyzing vast amounts of data often entail gathering sensitive personal information. Organizations must tread carefully to maintain user privacy and comply with stringent data protection regulations. Balancing between comprehensive data analysis for security purposes and safeguarding individual privacy presents a delicate challenge.

Another aspect is the scalability of infrastructure. Effective big data analytics in cybersecurity requires scalable solutions to handle increasing data volumes. Traditional infrastructures often struggle to scale efficiently, making it necessary to invest in more sophisticated technologies like distributed computing and cloud services. However, migrating to advanced infrastructures comes with its own set of challenges, including costs and transition complexities.

Big data analytics systems are also susceptible to become an attack vector themselves. Cybercriminals may target data storage systems, aiming to corrupt or steal valuable data. Ensuring the robustness and security of these analytics systems is crucial to avoid becoming victims of the very threats we're trying to detect and mitigate.

Interoperability issues can arise when integrating different big data technologies and cybersecurity tools. Various systems and tools might not seamlessly work together, causing data silos and inefficiencies. Achieving seamless integration and interoperability among different technologies demands careful planning and investment in compatible solutions.

Additionally, ethical considerations abound in big data use within cybersecurity. The need to collect extensive data for analysis often clashes with ethical norms concerning user consent and data use. Organizations need to adopt transparent data collection policies, seek user consent, and maintain ethical standards while ensuring robust cybersecurity measures.

Decision-making based on big data analytics can be challenging. The accuracy and reliability of insights derived from big data hinge on the quality of the underlying data and the efficacy of analytic algorithms. Misinterpretations or errors in data analysis can lead to poor decision-making, affecting an organization's cybersecurity posture.

Another notable challenge involves data storage and retention. The increasing volume of data necessitates significant storage capacities, escalating costs. Determining the appropriate duration for data retention that balances between historical analysis capabilities and cost-efficiencies remains a contentious issue. Over-retention can be as problematic as under-retention, affecting operational agility and increasing vulnerabilities.

Finally, compliance with evolving regulatory frameworks adds another layer of complexity. Data protection laws vary across jurisdictions, and organizations need to stay updated with regulatory changes to avoid legal repercussions. Ensuring compliance involves continuous monitoring, adaptive policies, and regular audits, requiring dedicated resources and efforts.

In conclusion, while leveraging big data in cybersecurity offers unprecedented opportunities for enhanced threat detection and prevention, it is not without its challenges. Organizations must navigate the complexities of data volume, variety, quality, and privacy while ensuring robust infrastructure, skilled personnel, and ethical use. Overcoming these challenges is critical to unlocking the full potential of big data in safeguarding the digital realm.

Chapter 8:
AI and Cloud Security

As organizations increasingly migrate their operations to the cloud, the security landscape transforms, necessitating advanced AI-driven solutions for robust protection. Traditional security measures often fall short in addressing the dynamic and scalable nature of cloud environments. AI steps in by offering intelligent, adaptive defenses tailored to the complexity of cloud architectures. These AI solutions leverage machine learning algorithms to detect anomalies, predict potential threats, and automate responses, ensuring data integrity and privacy in real-time. By continually learning from vast datasets, AI enhances the detection of sophisticated cloud-based threats, ranging from unauthorized access to sophisticated malware. The integration of AI in cloud security not only fortifies defenses but also streamlines compliance with evolving regulatory standards. In essence, AI empowers businesses to embrace the cloud's full potential without compromising on security, setting a new paradigm in digital defense.

Security in the Cloud Environment

Shifting essential services and data to the cloud offers numerous benefits, from cost savings to increased flexibility. However, as organizations migrate to these cloud-based infrastructures, they also face new security challenges. Cloud environments, by their nature, introduce a different set of vulnerabilities and attack surfaces compared to traditional on-premise systems.

To begin with, the shared responsibility model in cloud security is one area that can't be ignored. In this model, cloud service providers (CSPs) and customers have distinct obligations. CSPs generally handle the security of the cloud, encompassing infrastructure, storage, and network elements. In contrast, customers are responsible for security in the cloud, managing operations such as application-level security, data encryption, and user access management. The line at which these duties meet is crucial, demanding a comprehensive understanding from both parties to avoid breaches due to misconfiguration and miscommunication.

The elasticity and scalability of cloud resources also pose unique challenges. For instance, auto-scaling can lead to temporary resources that might escape routine security audits and compliance checks. Ensuring these dynamic resources adhere to security policies requires sophisticated orchestration and automated compliance tools. Without meticulous oversight, orphaned resources can become points of vulnerability, easily exploitable by malicious actors.

One of the potent threats in the cloud ecosystem is data breaches. Unlike traditional systems, where data is mostly static, cloud environments often involve a high level of data mobility. Data can traverse multiple virtual machines, across various geographical zones, making it more susceptible to interception and theft. Techniques such as multi-tendency isolation, where different tenants operate on shared resources, further elevate the risk profile. Hence, robust encryption protocols, both in transit and at rest, are imperative for safeguarding data.

Additionally, insider threats remain a significant concern. With cloud access conveniently available through the internet, credential theft or misuse by insiders can lead to catastrophic consequences. Multi-factor authentication (MFA) and stringent identity and access management (IAM) practices are essential in mitigating these risks. Role-based access control (RBAC) and the principle of least privilege should be standard practices to ensure that users gain access only to the resources necessary for their roles.

Moreover, Distributed Denial of Service (DDoS) attacks present distinct challenges in cloud environments. The vast amount of resources in a cloud infrastructure may offer some inherent resilience, yet they also attract larger-scale DDoS attacks targeting the expanded attack surfaces. CSPs typically provide anti-DDoS services, but organizations need to understand the layered approach required—often combining provider solutions with additional safeguards tailored to specific needs.

Another critical aspect involves the API security. Cloud environments rely heavily on APIs for service provisioning, management, and monitoring. However, these APIs can be prime targets for attackers. Insecure APIs can lead to unauthorized access and data exposure. Ensuring that APIs are secured through strong authentication, authorization mechanisms, and regular security assessments is crucial. API gateways can serve as enforcement points to monitor and control API traffic, adding an additional layer of security.

Compliance and regulatory requirements in the cloud add another layer of complexity. Different industries have distinct regulations such as GDPR for data protection in the EU or HIPAA for healthcare information in the U.S. Maintaining compliance in a constantly adapting cloud environment requires continuous monitoring and regular audits. Tools and services that offer continuous compliance can help organizations stay compliant by automatically adjusting to the latest regulatory demands.

Security Information and Event Management (SIEM) systems are also proving to be invaluable in cloud security. These systems aggregate logs and events from various sources such as applications, network gear, and endpoints. When integrated with AI capabilities, SIEM systems provide improved anomaly detection, identifying suspicious activities that may indicate a breach. AI-driven SIEM tools can analyze vast amounts of data in real-time, offering timely alerts and enabling faster incident responses.

Vulnerability management in the cloud environment presents unique hurdles, especially with ephemeral resources like containers and serverless functions. Traditional vulnerability scanners may not fully understand the transient nature of such resources, leading to gaps in security assessments. Modern solutions leverage AI to improve the accuracy and speed of vulnerability detection, adapting to the dynamic nature of cloud technologies.

Keeping cloud resources up-to-date with patches is another significant consideration. Cloud environments might host numerous services and applications, each with its own set of dependencies. Automated patch management systems, driven by AI, can significantly reduce the burden on security teams, ensuring timely updates without manual intervention. These systems can prioritize patches based on the severity of vulnerabilities, facilitating a proactive approach to threat mitigation.

Disaster recovery and business continuity plans also require a tailored approach in the cloud. With data and services distributed across multiple locations, ensuring a rapid and effective response to disasters is crucial. Automated failover mechanisms and regular disaster recovery drills are essential components. AI-driven analytics can help in predicting potential failures and guiding the resource allocation for resilient operations.

Finally, continuous education and training of personnel managing cloud environments can't be understated. As cloud technologies evolve, the security landscape changes alongside them. Regular training sessions, certification programs, and up-to-date knowledge repositories can empower teams to stay ahead of new threats and vulnerabilities. AI-powered learning platforms can offer customized training modules, based on emerging trends and individual knowledge gaps.

In essence, securing the cloud environment demands a nuanced approach, intertwined with robust technologies and proactive strategies. As organizations increasingly rely on cloud services, understanding and addressing the distinct security requirements is imperative. Embracing AI-driven solutions and best practices ensures that cloud resources remain secure, resilient, and compliant, paving the way for a secure digital transformation.

Cloud-Based Threats

The advent of cloud computing has revolutionized the way organizations handle data, offering unprecedented flexibility and scalability. However, as with any technological advancement, it also introduces a new array of security threats. When data travels between on-premises infrastructure and cloud environments, it becomes vulnerable to various attacks. This section delves into the complexities and perils of cloud-based threats, amplifying the importance of robust AI-driven security solutions.

One of the fundamental threats in cloud environments is data breaches. With sensitive information stored offsite, often by third-party providers, unauthorized access becomes a focal point of concern. Cybercriminals target cloud storage systems attempting to exploit vulnerabilities in authentication mechanisms or employee mishaps. The stakes are incredibly high—once a data breach occurs, it can result in not only financial losses but also irreversible damage to an organization's reputation.

Insider threats add another layer of complexity. Employees with access to critical systems might intentionally or unintentionally expose sensitive data. In traditional IT setups, monitoring such activities is challenging, but in a cloud environment, it's even more so. Disgruntled employees can quickly become dangerous insiders, misusing their access to cloud resources, potentially causing significant damage before being identified and neutralized.

Cloud misconfigurations are a perilous yet surprisingly common issue. These occur when cloud resources aren't configured securely, inadvertently leaving data exposed. Simple errors in setting access permissions, encryption settings, or network configurations can create vulnerabilities. Threat actors can then exploit these weaknesses to gain unauthorized access or deploy malware. Misconfigurations have been at the root of some high-profile security lapses, making it an issue organizations must vigilantly guard against.

Denial-of-Service (DoS) attacks are yet another method cybercriminals use to disrupt cloud services. By overwhelming cloud servers with a flood of illegitimate requests, attackers can effectively shut down services, denying access to legitimate users. This not only affects operational efficiency but can also erode customer trust. Distributed Denial-of-Service (DDoS) attacks add a layer of complexity by utilizing multiple compromised systems to target cloud infrastructure, raising the bar for resilience strategies.

Multi-tenant environments in the cloud pose unique security risks. Here, different organizations share the same hardware and storage resources. If a cyber attacker is able to compromise one tenant, there's the potential for a "side-channel" attack where other tenants' data or resources could become accessible. This inter-tenant threat highlights the critical need for hyper-secure isolation mechanisms within cloud platforms.

APIs are crucial for cloud services, enabling software interactions and automated operations. However, they're also prime targets for attackers. *API Security* vulnerabilities can expose sensitive data or provide entry points for launching attacks. Hackers often look for poorly protected APIs to exploit, and once they succeed, they can execute commands, extract data, or even hijack entire cloud resources.

Man-in-the-cloud attacks represent another sophisticated threat vector. Here, attackers focus on the synchronization tokens used by cloud services to legitimize user sessions. Once the attacker intercepts this token, they can gain unauthorized access to cloud repositories, often bypassing traditional security measures. It's a subtle yet highly effective way to infiltrate cloud infrastructure without triggering immediate alarms.

The proliferation of Bring Your Own Device (BYOD) policies introduces significant cloud-based threats as well. Employees accessing company data from their personal devices often bypass stringent security measures, creating weak links. Malware can easily find its way onto personal devices and then leverage these unsecured endpoints to infiltrate corporate cloud resources. This necessitates a harmonious balance between operational flexibility and robust security protocols.

Cloud-based threats extend beyond mere data and system attacks; they also include hybrid cloud vulnerabilities. Organizations frequently utilize a mix of public, private, and hybrid clouds to meet diverse needs. Each setup has distinct security challenges. For instance, data movement between different environments can create encryption and access control complexities. An attacker exploiting a vulnerability in one part of a hybrid cloud setup can eventually breach the entire ecosystem, making holistic security strategies imperative.

Another concern comes from the rapid evolution of threat landscapes, often outpacing the traditional security measures in place. Cyber adversaries continually innovate, deploying advanced techniques like polymorphic malware, which frequently changes its code to evade detection. Adding AI to security frameworks significantly counters this, providing real-time analysis and adaptive defensive measures.

In the context of cloud-based threats, AI can play a multifaceted role. AI-driven anomaly detection systems, for instance, can monitor traffic patterns and user behaviors in real-time, quickly identifying deviations that may indicate a security breach. Machine learning algorithms can be trained to recognize the subtle indicators of insider threats, potentially stopping malicious activity before it can do extensive harm. Automation enabled by AI helps ensure misconfigurations are detected and corrected promptly, reducing risks associated with human error.

Also, leveraging large datasets aggregated across multiple cloud environments allows AI to offer predictive insights. Predictive analytics can forecast potential attacks, enabling organizations to fortify defenses proactively. For example, if AI identifies a specific type of attack trend in the infrastructure of different organizations, it can suggest preemptive actions. This proactive defense mechanism is especially crucial in the dynamic, ever-evolving threat landscape of the cloud.

Finally, encryption is indispensable in cloud security. End-to-end encryption ensures data remains secure during its entire lifecycle—both at rest and in transit. AI enhances encryption strategies by dynamically adjusting encryption keys and protocols based on real-time threat assessments. This continuous adaptation ensures that encryption mechanisms aren't static targets but ever-adapting defense shields, thus providing a more robust safeguard against potential breaches.

In summarizing the landscape of cloud-based threats, it's clear that while cloud computing offers immense operational benefits, it also requires dedicated security measures tailored to its unique challenges. AI stands out as an essential element in modern cloud security strategies, providing dynamic, scalable solutions to these evolving threats. As we delve deeper into AI solutions for cloud security in the next section, it's evident that integrating AI can offer unparalleled enhancements to your cybersecurity posture.

AI Solutions for Cloud Security

As enterprises increasingly migrate their data and applications to the cloud, ensuring the security of these environments becomes paramount. The complexities of cloud infrastructure and the dynamic nature of cloud services necessitate a more advanced approach to cybersecurity. Enter Artificial Intelligence (AI), which offers innovative solutions tailored to tackle the unique challenges posed by cloud security. In this section, we'll delve into how AI is revolutionizing cloud security, the mechanisms employed, and the benefits conferred.

One of the primary advantages of AI in cloud security is its ability to continuously monitor vast amounts of data in real-time. Unlike traditional security systems that might only perform occasional checks, AI systems remain vigilant 24/7. They can detect anomalies quickly, often before any damage occurs. These systems leverage machine learning algorithms to learn what "normal" behavior looks like within a cloud environment. When deviations from the norm are detected, alerts are immediately generated, and if configured, defensive actions are automatically taken.

Beyond merely observing, AI has proven particularly adept at predictive analytics. Traditional security controls often operate reactively, addressing threats as they come. In contrast, AI systems can anticipate potential vulnerabilities and attack vectors. By analyzing historical data and threat patterns, AI models can forecast which areas of a cloud infrastructure are most likely to be targeted. This allows organizations to fortify these areas proactively, mitigating threats before they manifest.

Moreover, AI-driven Intrusion Detection Systems (IDS) in the cloud offer capabilities that far surpass their traditional counterparts. Network-based IDS and Host-based IDS can be significantly enhanced with AI, allowing for more nuanced and accurate threat detection. These systems can identify and block sophisticated attacks that might slip through conventional defenses. By employing deep learning techniques, AI can scrutinize traffic patterns, user behaviors, and even encrypted data streams for signs of malicious activity without significant latency, ensuring smooth operational continuity.

AI also excels in automating routine security tasks, freeing up human resources for more strategic activities. Automated patch management is a prime example. In the cloud, where new vulnerabilities can emerge rapidly due to the interconnected nature of services, timely patching is crucial. AI can autonomously identify outdated software, retrieve the necessary patches, and apply them across the entire cloud environment with minimal disruption. This automation reduces the window of vulnerability and ensures that systems remain up-to-date without manual intervention.

Additionally, AI and Natural Language Processing (NLP) have introduced sophisticated tools for managing cloud security policies. Given the vast array of configurable options in cloud environments, ensuring that security policies are correctly set is a daunting task. NLP-driven tools can interpret human language and translate it into enforceable security policies. For instance, administrators can describe desired security states in plain English, and the AI system can implement the corresponding technical configurations. This not only streamlines the process but also reduces the likelihood of misconfigurations.

Another critical area where AI is making a difference is in securing multi-cloud and hybrid cloud environments. These environments, characterized by their use of multiple cloud service providers and integration with on-premise infrastructure, present unique security challenges. AI algorithms can bridge the security gaps between disparate systems, ensuring unified threat detection and response. They enable a holistic view of the security posture across all platforms, ensuring no area is left vulnerable.

Privacy and compliance are integral to cloud security, and here too, AI offers invaluable assistance. Regulatory requirements such as GDPR, CCPA, and HIPAA mandate stringent data protection standards. AI can aid in achieving and maintaining compliance by continuously auditing cloud environments, identifying non-compliant areas, and recommending or executing corrective actions. Machine learning models can also help in data classification, ensuring sensitive information is appropriately safeguarded and access is strictly controlled.

Simultaneously, it's important to consider the role of AI in disaster recovery and business continuity planning. In the event of a security breach or failure within a cloud environment, swift response and recovery are crucial. AI-driven incident response systems can automatically initiate predefined recovery protocols, minimizing downtime and data loss. Furthermore, these systems can learn from past incidents, continually improving their response strategies to better protect against future threats.

However, leveraging AI for cloud security isn't without challenges. One significant concern is the reliance on data quality and volume. AI systems are only as good as the data they are trained on. Poor quality or insufficient data can lead to inaccurate predictions and false positives or negatives. Therefore, organizations must ensure that their AI models are fed with comprehensive, high-quality data to maximize efficacy.

Another challenge is the potential for AI systems themselves to become targets. Cyber adversaries are increasingly aware of the capabilities of AI and may attempt to deceive or corrupt these systems. Ensuring the resilience and integrity of AI models is critical. Techniques such as adversarial training, where models are exposed to malicious data during training to bolster their robustness, can be employed to enhance resilience.

Despite these challenges, the advantages of AI in cloud security are undeniable. The ability to operate at scale, provide real-time insights, and automate security operations positions AI as a cornerstone of modern cloud security strategies. Organizations that effectively integrate AI into their cloud security frameworks will likely find themselves better equipped to handle current and future threats.

In conclusion, AI offers a transformative approach to cloud security, addressing the unique and complex challenges posed by these environments. From real-time monitoring and predictive analytics to automated patch management and compliance auditing, AI provides comprehensive and adaptive solutions. As AI technology continues to evolve, its role in cloud security will undoubtedly expand, ushering in an era of enhanced digital defense. The stakes are high, but with AI on our side, the balance of power in cloud security stands firmly in our favor.

Chapter 9:
Case Studies of AI in Cyber Defense

In recent years, artificial intelligence has been the linchpin that many cybersecurity professionals have relied upon to fend off increasingly sophisticated cyber threats. This chapter delves into compelling case studies showcasing how AI enhances cyber defense. From financial institutions using machine learning to detect fraudulent transactions in real time, to tech giants deploying AI-driven intrusion detection systems that adapt and evolve with every threat encountered, the applications are both diverse and effective. One notable success story involves a healthcare provider that integrated natural language processing with anomaly detection, successfully mitigating phishing attacks targeting sensitive patient data. These real-world examples not only highlight the successes but also underscore important lessons learned, including the necessity for constant evolution and adaptation in AI algorithms to outpace cybercriminals. This evidence-based exploration aims to provide readers with actionable insights into the transformative power of AI in digital defense.

Real-World Applications

Artificial Intelligence (AI) has moved beyond theoretical discussions and academic papers, making tangible impacts in the realm of cybersecurity. One of the most prominent real-world applications of AI in cyber defense is in enhancing the capabilities of Intrusion Detection Systems (IDS). Traditionally, IDS relied on predefined rules and signatures to identify malicious activities, which made them vulnerable to new and unknown threats. AI has revolutionized this by using machine learning algorithms that can recognize patterns and anomalies that signify potential intrusions. In practice, these AI-driven IDS can detect zero-day exploits and sophisticated attacks that traditional systems would likely miss.

Another significant application of AI in cybersecurity is in the automation of security operations. Security Operation Centers (SOCs) are often overwhelmed with the sheer volume of alerts and potential threats that come through their systems daily. AI can sift through this data at a scale and speed unattainable by human analysts, prioritizing threats and automatically initiating responses. This ensures quicker reactions to genuine threats, reducing the window of opportunity for attackers. By automating repetitive and data-intensive tasks, AI enables human analysts to focus on more complex decision-making processes, thereby improving overall efficiency and effectiveness.

Predictive analytics powered by AI has also found a pivotal role in cyber defense. By analyzing vast amounts of historical data, AI systems can predict potential security incidents before they occur. This proactive approach is especially critical in sectors like finance and healthcare, where data breaches can have catastrophic consequences. For example, AI algorithms analyze transaction patterns to flag potentially fraudulent activities even before they result in financial loss. Similarly, in healthcare, AI can predict potential breaches based on unusual access patterns to sensitive patient data, thereby preempting the compromise of confidential information.

In addition to detection and prevention, AI is making inroads in cybersecurity through its superior capabilities in natural language processing (NLP). NLP allows AI systems to process and understand human language in emails, messages, and social media posts. This capability is especially useful in combating phishing attacks, which often rely on tricking users into revealing confidential information. AI algorithms can scan incoming emails for phishing red flags, such as suspicious links or atypical language patterns, and either flag them for review or block them entirely. This real-time filtering helps prevent users from falling victim to social engineering attacks.

Another compelling application of AI in cybersecurity is in endpoint protection. Traditional antivirus software required regular updates to recognize new threats, but AI-driven antivirus solutions can learn and adapt without constant manual input. These advanced systems continuously monitor the behavior of applications and files on a device, recognizing and neutralizing threats based on their behavior rather than relying solely on known signatures. In practice, this means better protection against polymorphic malware and other evolving threats that change their code to evade detection.

One of the often overlooked but vital applications of AI in cybersecurity is in risk assessment. AI can aggregate data from multiple sources—network logs, user behavior analytics, threat intelligence feeds—to provide a comprehensive risk profile for an organization. This holistic view enables companies to identify vulnerabilities and address them proactively. For instance, AI can analyze open-source intelligence and dark web chatter to alert companies about potential targeted attacks on their infrastructure, allowing them to beef up defenses ahead of time.

AI's role in cyber forensics is also noteworthy. Investigating cyber incidents often requires analyzing extensive data logs to pinpoint the origin and method of an attack. AI tools can significantly expedite this process by identifying relevant patterns and relationships within the data, helping forensic analysts draw conclusions faster. Machine learning algorithms sift through log data, highlighting anomalies that human analysts might miss. This not only accelerates the investigative process but also improves the accuracy of the findings.

Beyond traditional IT environments, AI is making strides in securing the Internet of Things (IoT). IoT devices, with their perpetual connectivity and diversity, present unique security challenges. AI can help manage these challenges by monitoring the behavior of connected devices and identifying unusual patterns that might indicate a security breach. For example, an AI system could detect and quarantine a compromised smart thermostat participating in a botnet attack, thereby containing the threat before it escalates to other devices on the network.

AI's contribution to threat intelligence is another example of its real-world application. Threat intelligence involves collecting and analyzing data about existing and emerging threats to better defend against cyber attacks. AI models sift through vast amounts of data from various sources, such as hacker forums, dark web markets, and open-source intelligence, to identify potential threats and provide actionable insights. This enables organizations to stay ahead of attackers by understanding their tactics, techniques, and procedures (TTPs) and preparing accordingly.

Furthermore, AI-powered incident response systems are transforming how organizations handle security breaches. When a security incident occurs, time is of the essence. AI-enhanced response systems can automatically execute predefined response actions, such as isolating affected systems, alerting stakeholders, and rolling back malicious changes. This automation not only speeds up the incident response process but also reduces the room for human error, thereby ensuring a more effective and coordinated reaction to cyber threats.

Supply chain security is another area benefiting from AI applications in cybersecurity. Organizations today rely on complex supply chains involving numerous third-party vendors and partners. AI can monitor the security posture of these third parties by continuously scanning for vulnerabilities, assessing compliance with security standards, and detecting signs of data breaches or compromise. This level of vigilance helps organizations identify and mitigate risks arising from their supply chains, ensuring a more secure overall operational environment.

In the realm of compliance, AI is streamlining efforts to meet regulatory requirements. Many industries are subject to strict regulations regarding data protection and cybersecurity, such as GDPR, HIPAA, and CCPA. AI tools can automate the process of monitoring and auditing compliance by analyzing data handling practices, access logs, and communication patterns. This continuous compliance monitoring reduces the risk of regulatory violations and helps organizations prepare for audits more efficiently.

Lastly, AI's real-world applications extend to personalized user security. Customized security measures tailored to individual user behavior and preferences can significantly enhance protection. AI analyzes a user's typical behavior patterns to identify deviations that might indicate a compromised account. For example, if an AI system detects a login attempt from an unusual location or at an odd time, it can trigger additional authentication measures or alert the user. This personalized approach adds an extra layer of security, making it harder for malicious actors to exploit user accounts.

Success Stories

AI's remarkable influence on cybersecurity isn't just theoretical; it's proven in the field. With numerous success stories, we can see AI taking center stage in fending off cyber threats and streamlining defenses. Let's delve into some compelling examples that showcase the transformative power of AI in cyber defense.

One notable case is IBM's Watson for Cyber Security. Used by several large organizations, Watson employs natural language processing (NLP) to sift through vast amounts of data, identify potential threats, and provide actionable insights. For instance, a major financial institution integrated Watson into its security operations center (SOC). The outcome was staggering: it achieved a 60% reduction in response times and a significant decrease in false positives. Watson's ability to learn from every interaction means it continually improves, providing the financial institution with ever-better defenses against cyber threats.

Another illustrative example involves the cybersecurity firm Darktrace. Established by mathematicians and former government intelligence experts, Darktrace employs machine learning to detect threats in real time. A mid-sized healthcare provider leveraged Darktrace's Enterprise Immune System to combat ransomware attacks. Within weeks, the system identified a sophisticated attack attempting to exploit the provider's network through covert channels. The AI-driven insights enabled the IT team to neutralize the threat before any critical data was compromised. Subsequently, Darktrace's technology led to an 80% reduction in potential attack vectors for the healthcare provider.

The retail industry has also seen significant success with AI-driven cyber defenses. Take, for example, a global e-commerce platform that was continually besieged by bots staging credential stuffing attacks. These attacks aimed to gain unauthorized access using stolen login credentials. The company adopted a machine learning solution from a leading cybersecurity vendor, which specialized in anomaly detection. By identifying and blocking unusual login patterns, the incidence of successful breaches was drastically cut down. This not only saved the company from potential lawsuits and loss of customer trust but also preserved its market reputation.

In the telecommunications sector, companies have massive networks susceptible to varied cyber threats. One large telecom provider partnered with Palo Alto Networks to incorporate AI in its cybersecurity framework. Using deep learning algorithms, the company's system could predict and preemptively block DDoS attacks. Before leveraging AI, the provider endured frequent service interruptions, causing customer dissatisfaction. Post-AI integration, service uptime improved remarkably, providing uninterrupted service to millions of users. The predictive capability of AI allowed for a proactive approach to threat management, setting a new standard in the industry.

Corporate giants, like Microsoft, too have harnessed the power of AI for their internal cybersecurity measures. Utilizing machine learning and advanced analytics, Microsoft's security framework can process trillions of signals daily to identify threats. In one notable instance, their AI detected abnormal patterns in network traffic that traditional tools missed. These anomalies pointed to an advanced persistent threat (APT) targeting sensitive corporate data. Proactive AI interventions allowed Microsoft's security team to mitigate the risk promptly. This experience not only safeguarded crucial data but also showcased AI's potential in identifying sophisticated cyber threats.

Smaller businesses, often lacking extensive IT resources, aren't left out. They, too, are reaping benefits from AI-based solutions tailored to their needs. For example, a small law firm specializing in intellectual property was a frequent target of cyber attacks aimed at accessing client records. Adopting an AI-based intrusion detection system, the firm could monitor and analyze network activity in real time. This system not only identified and mitigated multiple intrusion attempts but also adjusted and improved its defenses over time. The firm reported a newfound peace of mind and increased client confidence knowing their data was secure.

Government agencies have also successfully implemented AI to bolster national security. The US Department of Defense employed AI systems to enhance threat prediction capabilities. These AI tools can analyze and synthesize data from numerous sources, including social media, satellite feeds, and internal databases. During an exercise, the AI system accurately forecasted potential cyber-attacks from adversary nation-states, allowing for pre-emptive measures. This capability has profoundly transformed how the Department approaches cyber defense, pivoting from reactive to proactive strategies.

Educational institutions, which often manage a treasure trove of sensitive information, have also turned to AI to maintain security. A leading university faced continuous threats of data breaches targeting student records and financial information. Implementing a comprehensive AI-driven security solution that incorporated machine learning and behavior analysis, the university drastically improved its ability to identify and respond to threats. Notably, the AI system detected and contained a breach attempt before any data could be exfiltrated, protecting the personal information of thousands of students.

The energy sector, critical to national infrastructure, has also seen AI's positive influence. One major utility company adopted an AI-based anomaly detection system to protect its industrial control systems (ICS). These systems are notoriously difficult to secure due to their legacy nature and operational demands. The AI solution continuously monitored network traffic and system behaviors, flagging any irregular patterns. In one instance, it identified an unusual data flow that turned out to be a precursor to a cyber-physical attack. The early detection averted what could have been a catastrophic failure in the energy grid, highlighting the importance of AI in critical infrastructure security.

Let's not forget the role of AI in protecting personal data. With the rise of smart home devices, individuals' private lives have become potential targets for cybercriminals. Companies like Symantec have developed AI-driven security systems for consumer use. One such system identified a malware strain attempting to infiltrate a homeowner's network through a smart thermostat. The AI promptly quarantined the threat, preventing unauthorized access to the homeowner's personal devices and data. This example underscores AI's expanding role in safeguarding not just large organizations but personal environments as well.

Success stories abound and serve as powerful testaments to AI's capability in transforming cybersecurity. By understanding these real-world applications, tech enthusiasts and cybersecurity professionals can grasp not just the theoretical aspects but the tangible, impactful results of AI in this critical field. As the landscape of digital threats continues to evolve, so too will the AI systems designed to combat them, ensuring a future where defense mechanisms stay one step ahead of cyber adversaries.

Lessons Learned

The application of Artificial Intelligence in cybersecurity has emerged as a powerful ally in combating digital threats. Through the exploration of various case studies, several critical lessons have come to the forefront. These lessons underscore the transformative potential of AI, as well as emphasizing the challenges and considerations that practitioners must navigate.

One of the most evident lessons is the value of proactive defense. Traditional cybersecurity measures have largely been reactive, addressing threats only after they have breached defenses. AI shifts this paradigm by enabling proactive measures such as predictive analytics and anomaly detection. When organizations employ AI to anticipate and mitigate threats before they materialize, the risk and impact of cyber attacks are significantly reduced.

Another key insight from these case studies is the importance of integrating AI with existing security frameworks. While AI offers advanced capabilities, its true potential is realized when seamlessly incorporated into the broader cybersecurity ecosystem. This ensures that AI-based tools can complement other technologies and practices, rather than operating in isolation. Consequently, organizations are better equipped to respond to the dynamic nature of cyber threats.

However, the deployment of AI in cyber defense also highlighted the continuous need for human oversight. Despite the sophistication of AI algorithms, human judgment remains indispensable. AI can efficiently handle massive volumes of data, identify patterns, and flag anomalies, but it is up to skilled cybersecurity professionals to interpret these findings and make informed decisions. This collaboration between human intelligence and artificial intelligence forms a robust defense mechanism.

The importance of data quality cannot be overstated. AI systems rely heavily on accurate, relevant, and timely data to perform effectively. Case studies revealed instances where inadequate or poor quality data led to erroneous conclusions and ineffective defenses. Therefore, rigorous data management practices are crucial to harness the full capabilities of AI.

Another lesson learned is the necessity of scalable solutions. Cyber threats continue to grow in both volume and complexity, necessitating scalable AI solutions that can adapt and grow alongside these evolving challenges. Organizations must prioritize AI tools that offer scalability to ensure long-term effectiveness and resilience.

Privacy concerns emerged as a recurring theme throughout the case studies. The use of AI in cybersecurity involves extensive data collection and analysis, which can raise privacy issues. Balancing strong security measures with the preservation of privacy requires meticulous planning and ethical considerations. Organizations need to develop strategies that respect user privacy while maximizing security.

Moreover, the importance of continuous learning and adaptation cannot be ignored. Cyber threats are not static; they evolve in sophistication and technique. AI systems, therefore, must be designed for continuous learning and improvement. Case studies demonstrated that static AI models become obsolete quickly, while adaptive systems remain effective by constantly learning from new data.

Integrating AI also necessitates a multidisciplinary approach. The complexity of deploying AI in cybersecurity cannot be underestimated. It requires expertise not only in cybersecurity but also in machine learning, data science, and domain-specific knowledge. Teams need to draw from a breadth of expertise to design, implement, and refine AI-driven security measures effectively.

From a strategic perspective, collaboration and information sharing among organizations emerged as a critical factor. Cybersecurity is not a zero-sum game, and the collective effort of sharing threat intelligence and best practices can lead to more robust defenses. AI systems benefit from diverse data sources, and collaboration accelerates the sharing of these valuable data sets.

The ethical deployment of AI also featured prominently in the lessons learned. Bias in AI algorithms can lead to unjust outcomes and compromise the fairness and effectiveness of cybersecurity measures. Developing ethical AI involves recognizing and mitigating biases, incorporating fairness into algorithms, and ensuring transparency and accountability in AI-driven decisions.

Finally, the significance of regulatory compliance was underscored in several case studies. As governments and international bodies introduce regulations governing the use of AI and data in cybersecurity, organizations must stay abreast of these legal requirements. Compliance not only avoids legal repercussions but also builds trust with stakeholders by demonstrating a commitment to responsible AI practices.

In summary, the integration of AI into cyber defense offers transformative benefits, but it is not without challenges. Proactive approaches, seamless integration, human oversight, data quality, scalability, privacy, continuous learning, a multidisciplinary approach, collaboration, ethical considerations, and regulatory compliance constitute the lessons learned. Each of these lessons contributes to a more resilient, efficient, and ethical application of AI in cybersecurity, paving the way for a safer digital future.

Chapter 10:
Ethical Considerations and Challenges

As AI continues to integrate into cybersecurity, the ethical landscape becomes increasingly complex, presenting a myriad of challenges that professionals can't ignore. Ensuring that AI systems operate ethically involves addressing key issues like bias and fairness, which can inadvertently lead to discriminatory practices if not properly managed. Privacy concerns also loom large, as AI's capability to analyze vast amounts of data raises questions about user consent and data ownership. Balancing these ethical considerations with the relentless pace of technological advancement requires a proactive approach and robust frameworks, ensuring that AI-driven cybersecurity solutions protect not only data but also the rights and freedoms of individuals. Addressing these challenges head-on is essential to fostering trust and promoting responsible AI adoption in the digital defense realm.

Ethical AI in Cybersecurity

Navigating the realm of ethical AI in cybersecurity isn't just about implementing robust defenses; it's about doing so responsibly and thoughtfully. Ethical considerations ensure AI technologies not only enhance security but also respect fundamental human values. This dimension of AI extends beyond technicalities, touching on societal implications.

One of the foremost ethical questions in cybersecurity is how to balance security needs with individual privacy. AI-driven systems can process an enormous amount of data to identify and neutralize threats. However, the same capability raises concerns regarding surveillance and data misuse. It's crucial to design AI systems that respect privacy by leveraging techniques like differential privacy, where data is anonymized and aggregated to prevent individual identification while still allowing for meaningful analysis.

Transparency in AI algorithms is another critical issue. AI models are often criticized for being "black boxes" where decision-making processes are opaque. This lack of transparency can lead to mistrust, especially if AI systems make high-stakes decisions that impact users. Ensuring that AI models are interpretable and their decisions understandable is essential. This is particularly true in cybersecurity, where stakeholders need to grasp why specific actions are taken to mitigate threats. Explainable AI (XAI) can help in making these processes more transparent, offering insights into how decisions are reached and fostering trust among users.

Bias in AI algorithms is a significant ethical challenge. Bias can stem from training data that does not adequately represent all user demographics or from the design of the algorithms themselves. In cybersecurity, biased AI can lead to skewed threat assessments, potentially overlooking threats to certain groups or overemphasizing threats to others. This can exacerbate existing inequalities and result in unfair treatment. To counteract this, it's important to use diverse datasets and continuously monitor AI systems for signs of bias, implementing adjustments as necessary to ensure fairness and accuracy.

The issue of accountability is also paramount. AI systems can make automated decisions that have significant consequences. When an AI system identifies a potential cyber threat and takes action, who is responsible if something goes wrong? Assigning accountability in AI-driven processes is complex but necessary to ensure ethical standards are maintained. Establishing clear guidelines and accountability frameworks helps in delineating responsibility, ensuring that developers, operators, and users understand their roles and the implications of AI actions.

Ethical AI also involves the consideration of how AI is used in offensive cybersecurity operations. While AI can significantly strengthen cyber defenses, the same technology can be weaponized to conduct attacks. This dual-use dilemma presents a moral quandary: enhancing defensive capabilities without contributing to the development of AI-driven offensive tools. Regulatory frameworks and international agreements can provide guidelines to ensure that AI is used ethically in the global landscape of digital defense.

Moreover, the deployment of AI in cybersecurity raises questions about the balance between automation and human oversight. While AI can significantly enhance efficiency and accuracy in threat detection and response, it's crucial to include human judgment in the loop to handle nuanced and complex situations. Humans provide contextual understanding and ethical discernment that AI might lack, making human-AI collaboration integral to an ethical cybersecurity strategy.

Ethical AI also touches upon the broader social impact of cybersecurity practices. Cybersecurity measures should not inadvertently marginalize certain groups or exacerbate digital divides. Ensuring equal access to robust cybersecurity solutions and fostering digital literacy across different demographics can mitigate these risks. Ethical AI should aim to empower all users, contributing to a more secure and equitable digital ecosystem.

Lastly, global collaboration and dialogue are essential in establishing and maintaining ethical standards for AI in cybersecurity. Cyber threats are a global concern, and so should be the ethical considerations of AI applications in this field. Encouraging international cooperation and sharing best practices can help harmonize ethical standards, ensuring that AI technology benefits society as a whole while minimizing potential harms. Initiatives like developing ethical guidelines, conducting ethical impact assessments, and fostering cross-border collaborations can be instrumental in this effort.

Ethical AI in cybersecurity is a multifaceted challenge that extends beyond technical proficiency to encompass a broader societal responsibility. By addressing issues like privacy, transparency, bias, accountability, and global collaboration, we can develop AI systems that not only safeguard our digital world but do so with integrity and fairness.

Bias and Fairness

When discussing bias and fairness within the realm of AI in cybersecurity, it's crucial to understand that these issues are not merely theoretical. They have practical implications which can significantly impact the effectiveness and trustworthiness of AI systems. AI systems used in cybersecurity must analyze vast amounts of data to detect anomalies, defend against threats, and respond to incidents. However, these systems are only as good as the data they are trained on and the algorithms that drive them.

Bias in AI systems often originates from the datasets used for training. For example, if an AI is trained on data that over-represents certain types of cyber-attacks but neglects others, it may be adept at detecting those specific attacks while missing or underperforming in recognizing others. This selective efficiency can lead to significant gaps in cybersecurity defenses. Additionally, bias can manifest in the way AI models are constructed and the assumptions that underpin them. For instance, an AI model might place undue weight on certain variables, skewing its predictions and responses in ways that are unfair or unbalanced.

While some biases are unintentional, they can still have serious ramifications. A biased AI could lead to an unequal focus on threats originating from particular geographic regions, thereby neglecting other regions and creating a false sense of security. Furthermore, such biases can compound over time, especially in systems that use continuous learning. If initial biases are not identified and corrected, the AI will perpetuate and possibly exacerbate them, further diminishing its fairness and effectiveness.

To tackle bias effectively, one must first employ rigorous testing methods during the development phase. This involves utilizing diverse datasets that include a wide array of cyber threats from different contexts and sources. Robust training datasets can help ensure the AI learns to recognize a varied spectrum of potential issues, reducing the risk of overlooking or undervaluing certain threats.

Another practical approach to mitigating bias involves continual monitoring and updating of AI systems. Regular audits and evaluations of AI performance should be conducted to spot disparities and rectify them promptly. Tools leveraging explainable AI (XAI) can be instrumental in this regard. These tools offer insights into how decisions are made within the AI system, enabling easier identification of biased behavior and underlying reasons.

However, technical solutions alone are not sufficient. Organizational culture also plays a fundamental role. Teams developing and managing these AI systems should be diverse in terms of background and experience to bring multiple perspectives to the table. This diversity can help anticipate and identify potential biases that a homogenous group might overlook. Moreover, ethical guidelines and training should be standard practice within these teams to cultivate an awareness of bias and fairness issues.

It's also worth noting that bias in AI isn't just a technological issue; it's a societal one. The perceptions and inherent biases in society can subtly influence the datasets and the AI models. For example, societal bias regarding gender or ethnicity can seep into the data, further perpetuating inequities if not adequately addressed. Thus, combating bias in AI requires continuous effort and an interdisciplinary approach involving technologists, ethicists, and sociologists.

Legal and regulatory frameworks also have a pivotal role in ensuring fairness. Governments and regulatory bodies need to establish and enforce robust standards for AI fairness in cybersecurity. These standards should outline the ethical use of AI, mandate transparency, and require accountability for biased outcomes. Compliance with these standards should not be seen as a mere legal obligation but as a core aspect of building trustworthy AI systems.

The need for ethical guidelines in the use of AI for cybersecurity can't be overstated. These guidelines should cover data collection practices, emphasizing the importance of obtaining diverse and representative datasets. Furthermore, they should stipulate regular audits and transparency in AI operations, requiring clear documentation of how decisions are made and ensuring that there are mechanisms for appeal or review.

Some organizations have started incorporating fairness audits as part of their AI lifecycle management. These audits assess whether the AI behaves consistently across different scenarios and demographics, identifying potential biases. They also examine whether the outcomes of AI-driven decisions are equitably distributed among various groups, ensuring no single group is unfairly disadvantaged.

An important concept to embrace is "fairness by design." This involves proactively designing AI systems with fairness as a primary objective rather than as an afterthought. Fairness by design necessitates integrating fairness considerations at every stage, from data collection and model training to deployment and continuous monitoring. This holistic approach is more effective than attempting to bolt fairness onto an already biased system.

Moreover, fairness is not a one-size-fits-all concept; it varies across different contexts and applications. In cybersecurity, fairness might mean ensuring all types of threats are given equal attention, irrespective of their origin, to protect a diverse array of users equally. It also entails providing equitable protections for all users, ensuring that AI defenses do not favor specific user groups over others.

The journey towards achieving bias-free and fair AI in cybersecurity is ongoing. It involves technical rigor, interdisciplinary collaboration, robust legal frameworks, and an unwavering commitment to ethics. By addressing these issues head-on, we can build AI systems that are not only effective in safeguarding our digital spaces but also equitable and just in their operations.

Privacy Concerns

In the realm of cybersecurity, privacy concerns are perhaps one of the most pressing issues. Artificial Intelligence (AI) has the potential to both enhance and compromise privacy. As AI systems become more sophisticated, they collect, process, and analyze vast amounts of data. This ability to handle large data sets can be a double-edged sword.

One immediate privacy concern with AI-driven cybersecurity is data collection. To detect anomalies and predict threats, AI systems require access to extensive data. This data often includes sensitive information such as personal identifiers, browsing habits, and communication logs. The question then arises: how do we ensure that this data is handled responsibly?

Another aspect of privacy concerns is data storage. AI systems need a place to store the vast amounts of data they collect. If these storage systems are not adequately secured, they become potential targets for cyber attacks themselves. We must consider what measures are in place to protect the data from unauthorized access, breaches, and leaks.

The need for transparency is pivotal. Users have a right to know how their data is being collected, processed, and used. However, many AI systems in cybersecurity operate in a "black box" manner. They make decisions based on complex algorithms that are not easily interpretable by humans. This lack of transparency can breed mistrust and raises ethical questions about accountability and oversight.

Moreover, the integration of AI in cybersecurity introduces the risk of data misuse. Unauthorized access to AI systems could allow malicious entities to manipulate the data or the AI's behavior. This misuse could lead to the compromise of sensitive information, exacerbating privacy breaches rather than preventing them.

Another layer of complexity is introduced with the evolution of AI technologies like Deep Learning and Natural Language Processing (NLP). These advanced techniques require even more data and computational resources. While they offer more precise threat detection and prevention, they also pose significant risks to data privacy. Deep Learning models can sometimes infer sensitive information from non-sensitive data, leading to unexpected privacy violations.

In addition, we must consider the ethical implications of mass surveillance enabled by AI in cybersecurity. While surveillance can be justified for security reasons, it can also infringe on individual privacy rights. Striking a balance between effective threat detection and respecting privacy rights is a delicate, ongoing challenge.

Consent is another critical point. Unlike traditional data collection methods, AI systems often collect data passively and automatically. Ensuring that users provide informed consent is complicated since they may not fully understand what they are consenting to. This problem is compounded by the fact that most users interact with AI systems indirectly, through various applications and services.

Then there's the issue of data anonymization. While anonymizing data can mitigate privacy risks, it is not foolproof. Sophisticated algorithms can sometimes re-identify individuals from anonymized data sets. Ensuring true anonymization is a complex task and often an unattainable ideal given current technological limitations.

Cross-border data transfers also complicate the privacy landscape. AI-driven cybersecurity systems often operate globally, collecting and analyzing data from numerous jurisdictions. However, privacy laws vary significantly around the world, leading to potential legal and ethical conflicts. Ensuring compliance with diverse regulations while maintaining the effectiveness of AI systems is a significant challenge.

An additional concern is the role of third-party vendors. Many organizations outsource parts of their cybersecurity to external service providers. These third parties might also use AI-driven systems to manage data. Ensuring that these vendors adhere to stringent privacy standards is essential but challenging, as it requires continuous monitoring and audits.

Furthermore, the issue of data minimization comes into play. Collecting only necessary data could help in mitigating privacy risks. However, defining "necessary" data is not always straightforward in the context of AI and cybersecurity. More data generally leads to more accurate AI predictions, but at what cost to privacy?

Regulatory frameworks and policies need to evolve to address these privacy concerns adequately. Policies need to be forward-looking, taking into account the rapid pace of AI development. They should focus on ensuring transparency, promoting accountability, and encouraging best practices in data handling and storage.

From a technical perspective, employing techniques like differential privacy and homomorphic encryption can help protect data in AI systems. Differential privacy adds "noise" to data to prevent the identification of individuals, while homomorphic encryption allows computations on encrypted data without exposing it. However, these techniques are not yet mature enough for widespread adoption in all applications.

Education and training are also crucial. Both developers and users of AI systems need to be aware of privacy implications and best practices. Regular training and updated guidelines could help mitigate privacy risks by fostering a culture of privacy-first thinking.

Finally, public engagement and discourse are needed to shape the future of AI in cybersecurity. Stakeholders, including technologists, policymakers, and the public, should engage in ongoing dialogue to address these complex privacy issues. This collaborative approach can lead to more balanced and effective solutions that protect both security and privacy.

In summary, as AI continues to revolutionize cybersecurity, it brings along substantial privacy concerns that must be carefully navigated. Ensuring transparent data practices, robust security measures, informed consent, and international cooperation are vital. By addressing these concerns thoughtfully and proactively, we can harness the power of AI while safeguarding individual privacy.

Chapter 11:
Regulatory and Legal Aspects

As the landscape of cybersecurity advances with AI-driven innovations, it becomes imperative to navigate the complexities of regulatory and legal frameworks. The integration of AI into cybersecurity introduces a new set of compliance requirements that organizations must adhere to, spanning diverse jurisdictions and industry-specific mandates. Global regulations, such as the GDPR in Europe and CCPA in California, set stringent standards for data protection and privacy, pushing entities to employ robust AI technologies for compliance. The evolving nature of cyber threats also demands that legal systems continuously adapt; thus, influencing the future of cyber law. Emerging legislation will likely focus on both the capabilities and limitations of AI, ensuring that while harnessing AI's potential, ethical boundaries and legal safeguards remain in place to protect individuals and organizations alike. Understanding these regulatory and legal aspects is crucial for cybersecurity professionals and tech enthusiasts aiming to leverage AI responsibly and effectively.

Compliance Requirements

Compliance in the realm of cybersecurity entails adhering to a broad spectrum of regulatory mandates and standards designed to ensure data protection, privacy, and the overall security of cyber infrastructures. For entities leveraging Artificial Intelligence (AI) in their cybersecurity measures, understanding and meeting these requirements is both a legal obligation and a critical element in maintaining trust with stakeholders. Laws such as the General Data Protection Regulation (GDPR) in Europe, the California Consumer Privacy Act (CCPA) in the United States, and sector-specific mandates like the Health Insurance Portability and Accountability Act (HIPAA) in healthcare create a complex web of compliance directives that organizations must navigate.

One key aspect of compliance is ensuring transparency and accountability, especially considering the use of AI's "black box" algorithms. Regulators demand that organizations can explain how these AI systems arrive at decisions or predictions, particularly when they impact individuals' data or security. This means companies must develop ways to provide insights into their machine learning models and algorithms without compromising proprietary technologies. In particular, the GDPR's "Right to Explanation" is a prime example of this requirement, compelling organizations to give clear, intelligible information about the logic involved in automated decisions.

Moreover, the compliance landscape is dynamically evolving. Governments and regulatory bodies continuously update laws and guidelines to keep pace with technological advancements. For instance, the introduction of new AI-specific regulations is increasingly becoming a focal point. The European Union's proposed AI regulation, known as the Artificial Intelligence Act, aims to set a precedent by categorizing AI systems based on their risk levels and setting compliance standards accordingly. As such, organizations must stay abreast of regulatory changes, which necessitates a proactive compliance strategy.

The stakes for non-compliance are exceptionally high. Financial penalties, legal repercussions, and reputational damage can follow lapses in meeting regulatory stipulations. A glaring example is the GDPR, which imposes fines up to 4% of a company's annual global turnover or €20 million (whichever is greater) for non-compliance. These stringent measures underline the importance of establishing rigorous compliance frameworks that are continually assessed and updated.

In terms of data handling, specific requirements from regulators often mandate data minimization, ensuring that only necessary data is collected and processed. Coupled with this are stipulations around data storage limitations and the necessity for data encryption both in transit and at rest. With AI systems often reliant on large datasets to train and validate models, striking a balance between these compliance mandates and operational efficacy can be challenging. Organizations must implement robust data governance protocols to manage and protect data in accordance with legal requirements.

Furthermore, compliance involves intricate documentation and record-keeping to demonstrate adherence to regulatory standards. This includes maintaining logs of data processing activities, evidence of consents obtained, and details of data protection impact assessments (DPIAs). These records must be readily available for auditing purposes, reflecting the organization's diligence in maintaining compliance.

It's also critical to include regular employee training programs focusing on compliance aspects. Educating employees on the importance of regulatory requirements and their role in upholding these standards helps create a culture of compliance. Additionally, given the rapid evolution of both cyber threats and countermeasures, ongoing training ensures that the workforce remains knowledgeable about current laws and best practices.

For organizations that operate across multiple jurisdictions, managing compliance can be doubly complex. Each region may have different regulations with unique stipulations and enforcement mechanisms. Multi-national companies need to adopt a harmonized approach that allows them to be compliant in all operating regions without duplicating efforts. This could involve establishing centralized compliance oversight that can implement location-specific adaptations as needed.

The interaction between AI and privacy laws introduces another layer of complexity. AI's capability to analyze massive datasets may inadvertently lead to privacy infringements if not properly managed. Complying with privacy regulations such as GDPR or CCPA requires careful planning to ensure AI systems respect individuals' rights to privacy, including the handling of sensitive information and adherence to data subject access requests (DSARs).

Lastly, third-party risk management is a vital component of compliance. When incorporating AI solutions provided by external vendors, organizations must ensure these third-party systems also comply with relevant regulations. This necessitates comprehensive vetting processes, ongoing assessments, and clear contractual obligations to uphold compliance requirements throughout the supply chain. Failure to manage third-party risks effectively can result in compliance breaches and associated penalties.

Overall, a strategic, proactive approach to compliance is crucial for organizations employing AI in cybersecurity. This involves continuously monitoring regulatory landscapes, updating policies and practices accordingly, and fostering an organizational culture that prioritizes compliance. By doing so, organizations can not only avoid penalties but also build trust with clients and stakeholders, ultimately fortifying their reputation in the industry.

Global Regulations

In the age of digital transformation and the proliferation of AI technologies in cybersecurity, governments worldwide are grappling with establishing coherent and effective regulatory frameworks. Global regulations are designed to ensure that AI-driven solutions are implemented ethically, securely, and responsibly.

Global cybersecurity regulations vary significantly from one region to another. The European Union (EU) has been a pioneer in establishing stringent data privacy and cybersecurity regulations through legislation like the General Data Protection Regulation (GDPR). GDPR not only focuses on the protection of personal data but also mandates strict security measures that organizations must follow to safeguard against cyber threats.

Meanwhile, in the United States, the regulatory landscape is more fragmented. Different sectors are governed by different regulations. For instance, the healthcare industry must comply with the Health Insurance Portability and Accountability Act (HIPAA), while the financial sector adheres to the Gramm-Leach-Bliley Act (GLBA). Each piece of legislation lays out specific guidelines for implementing cybersecurity measures, including the use of AI technologies.

The Asia-Pacific region presents a diverse and evolving regulatory environment. Countries like Singapore and Australia have proactively crafted regulations to address the cybersecurity challenges posed by AI. Singapore's Cybersecurity Act provides a robust framework for the protection of critical information infrastructure, reflecting its strong stance on cybersecurity. Australia's Security Legislation Amendment (Critical Infrastructure) Bill seeks to enhance the resilience of critical infrastructure against cyber threats, emphasizing the importance of cybersecurity measures.

In contrast, some regions are still in the nascent stages of developing comprehensive cybersecurity regulations. Latin American countries, for example, are beginning to recognize the need for stringent cybersecurity laws and the role of AI in enforcing them. Brazil's General Data Protection Law (LGPD) is a significant step towards harmonizing cybersecurity standards with international norms.

The regulatory landscape for AI in cybersecurity also includes multinational initiatives. The Budapest Convention on Cybercrime by the

Council of Europe serves as the first international treaty seeking to address Internet and computer crimes by harmonizing national laws and improving international cooperation. Although not explicitly focused on AI, the treaty provides a framework that can be adapted as AI technologies evolve.

Additionally, organizations such as the International Organization for Standardization (ISO) and the International Telecommunication Union (ITU) are working on global standards for AI and cybersecurity. These standards aim to establish a common language and guidelines that can be adopted by countries worldwide. ISO/IEC 27001, for instance, provides a framework for information security management systems (ISMS), which is crucial for integrating AI-driven cybersecurity measures.

Breaching global regulations can have severe consequences for organizations. Penalties can be financial or involve operational restrictions. GDPR, for example, imposes hefty fines for noncompliance, which can be as high as 4% of a company's global annual turnover. Such stringent measures aim to enforce a higher standard of cybersecurity practices, including the responsible use of AI technologies.

Despite the existence of numerous regulations, the fast-paced development of AI technologies presents ongoing challenges. Regulatory bodies often struggle to keep their policies current with the rapid advancements in AI. This lag creates a regulatory vacuum where technologies might outstrip governance, potentially leading to security vulnerabilities and ethical issues. Continuous review and adaptation of regulations are essential to keep pace with technological progress.

International cooperation is critical for effective global cybersecurity regulation. Cyber threats are, by nature, borderless and can originate from anywhere in the world. Collaboration between governments, international organizations, and the private sector can help create more comprehensive and unified regulations. Sharing best practices, threat intelligence, and regulatory frameworks can enhance the global cybersecurity posture against AI-driven threats.

Moreover, the ethical implications of AI in cybersecurity must be addressed within regulatory frameworks. Issues such as bias in AI algorithms, transparency of AI decision-making processes, and accountability need consideration. Regulatory bodies must ensure that AI systems in cybersecurity are not only effective but also fair and non-discriminatory.

The future of global regulations in cybersecurity will likely involve more dynamic and adaptive approaches. Policymakers are increasingly recognizing the need for regulations that can evolve alongside technological advancements. Regulatory sandboxes, which allow for the testing of AI technologies in a controlled environment, are becoming more popular as a means to develop and refine regulations before they are fully implemented.

In conclusion, global regulations play a crucial role in shaping the use of AI in cybersecurity. While significant strides have been made, ongoing collaboration and adaptation are necessary to address the complexities of AI technologies and the ever-evolving threat landscape. Countries must work together to develop coherent, comprehensive, and forward-looking regulations that ensure the secure and ethical use of AI in digital defense.

The Future of Cyber Law

The integration of AI into cybersecurity has brought significant benefits, but it has also pushed the boundaries of existing regulatory and legal frameworks. As technology rapidly evolves, cyber law must adapt to anticipate new challenges and address the complexities introduced by AI. The convergence of AI and cybersecurity will necessitate an agile, forward-thinking legal approach to adequately protect both individuals and organizations from emerging digital threats.

First, consider the rapid pace at which AI technology is developing. Traditional legal structures often struggle to keep up with technological advancements. This dynamic creates opportunities for malicious actors to exploit gaps in the law. Future cyber law must account for the speed of technological innovation, ensuring regulations are not just reactive but also proactively designed to address potential vulnerabilities.

One of the primary challenges in future cyber law will be defining liability when AI systems are involved. In an AI-driven cybersecurity landscape, determining responsibility for data breaches, unauthorized access, or cyber attacks may become increasingly complex. Who is accountable when an AI system fails to detect a threat or, worse yet, is subverted to carry out an attack? The answer isn't straightforward and will likely depend on a combination of factors, including the AI's level of autonomy and the foreseeability of the threat.

Moreover, the global nature of cyber threats complicates jurisdictional issues. Cyber attacks don't respect national borders, yet legal systems remain largely confined within them. Future cyber law will need to establish more robust frameworks for international cooperation, enabling countries to work together in combating sophisticated, cross-border cyber threats. This will likely involve the harmonization of cyber laws to ensure consistent legal standards and practices across different jurisdictions.

The use of AI in cybersecurity also raises significant privacy concerns. AI systems often require large datasets to function effectively, and the collection, storage, and analysis of this data must be carefully regulated to protect individuals' privacy rights. Future cyber law will need to strike a delicate balance between enabling the benefits of AI-powered cybersecurity solutions and safeguarding personal privacy.

This might entail stringent data protection regulations and comprehensive transparency requirements to ensure that the handling of personal data is both lawful and ethical.

Intellectual property laws will also face new challenges in the AI-driven cyber landscape. AI algorithms themselves, developed and refined for cybersecurity purposes, constitute valuable intellectual property. Future cyber law will need to provide clear guidelines on the ownership and protection of these algorithms to foster innovation while preventing misuse.

Ethical considerations are another critical aspect that future cyber law must address. With AI systems making autonomous decisions, ethical standards must be established to guide their development and deployment. This involves ensuring that AI systems are designed to avoid bias and discrimination, especially in sensitive areas like surveillance and threat detection. Legal frameworks will need to enforce these ethical standards, holding developers and organizations accountable for the ethical implications of their AI systems.

The rise of AI in cybersecurity also necessitates robust compliance frameworks. Organizations will need to adhere to regulatory standards that ensure the safe and ethical use of AI technologies. Future cyber law must outline comprehensive compliance requirements that cover the spectrum from data protection to algorithmic accountability. This will likely involve regular audits, certifications, and ongoing assessments to ensure that AI systems in cybersecurity remain compliant with established legal standards.

Finally, as we look ahead, future cyber law will have to be incredibly flexible and adaptive. The unpredictability of technological advancements means that legal frameworks cannot afford to be static. Instead, they will need to be continuously reviewed and updated to remain relevant and effective. This might involve the establishment of specialized regulatory bodies tasked with monitoring emerging technologies and recommending necessary legal adjustments.

In conclusion, the future of cyber law will be defined by its ability to navigate the complexities introduced by AI. It will need to address questions of liability, privacy, intellectual property, ethics, compliance, and international collaboration. As AI continues to shape the cybersecurity landscape, legal frameworks must evolve in tandem, ensuring that they provide robust protection against digital threats while fostering innovation and respecting individual rights. The adaptability and foresight of these legal frameworks will be crucial in securing a safe and resilient digital future.

Chapter 12:
The Future of AI in Cybersecurity

The future of AI in cybersecurity looks promising as emerging technologies continue to revolutionize the field. With advancements in machine learning, deep learning, and natural language processing, AI systems are becoming more adept at identifying and mitigating threats in real-time. Future trends suggest a shift towards more autonomous cybersecurity systems that can predict and counteract attacks before they occur. Additionally, as the complexity of cyber threats evolves, AI will play a crucial role in refining automated incident response and forensic systems, enhancing overall resilience. Preparing for tomorrow's threats means not just adopting these cutting-edge technologies but also addressing ethical considerations and regulatory compliance to ensure robust and fair defense mechanisms. This path forward mandates continuous innovation and collaboration between tech developers, cybersecurity professionals, and policymakers.

Emerging Technologies

When we talk about the future of AI in cybersecurity, it's crucial to consider the emerging technologies that are shaping this landscape. These technologies aren't just on the horizon; they're already knocking on the door and showing immense potential in revolutionizing how we approach cyber defense. From quantum computing to blockchain, new frontiers are opening up, each bringing its own set of capabilities and challenges.

One prominent emerging technology is quantum computing. This technology harnesses the principles of quantum mechanics to process information at unprecedented speeds and volumes. Traditional encryption methods, which rely on the difficulty of solving complex mathematical problems, could be rendered obsolete by quantum computers. While this presents a significant threat to current cybersecurity measures, it also offers new opportunities. Quantum cryptography, for instance, promises to create virtually unbreakable encryption through quantum key distribution (QKD). If adopted widely, QKD could become a cornerstone of future secure communications.

Another field making waves is edge computing. In contrast to cloud computing, which centralizes data processing, edge computing pushes data processing closer to the data source. This decentralization reduces latency and bandwidth usage, making real-time data processing more efficient. For cybersecurity, edge computing means that data can be analyzed and threats identified more quickly, thereby reducing the window of vulnerability. By integrating AI algorithms at the edge, systems can offer near-instantaneous responses to potential threats.

Blockchain technology, originally developed for cryptocurrencies, is also finding applications in cybersecurity. Blockchain's decentralized ledger system offers a transparent and immutable record of transactions, providing a robust framework for security. Smart contracts, which are self-executing contracts with the terms of the agreement directly written into code, could automate numerous security processes. For example, automated compliance checks and secure identity management are becoming possible uses of blockchain in cybersecurity.

In the realm of artificial intelligence itself, we're seeing the rise of federated learning. This technique allows AI models to be trained across multiple decentralized devices or servers while keeping data localized. By ensuring data doesn't all gather in one place, federated learning enhances security and privacy. It's a promising approach for sectors requiring stringent data confidentiality, like healthcare and finance. Federated learning also reduces the potential impact of a data breach since the data is distributed across multiple locations.

Biometric authentication is another emerging technology making significant strides. Fingerprints, facial recognition, and iris scans are becoming more common, offering enhanced security over traditional password systems. Biometric data is much harder to forge or steal, making it a reliable method for verifying identity. However, it's not without challenges. Privacy concerns and the risk of biometric data breaches still need to be addressed to maximize the benefits of this technology.

AI-powered deception technologies are also gaining traction. These systems use AI to create realistic decoys and traps, known as honeypots, to attract and detect cyber attackers. By analyzing the behavior of intruders in these controlled environments, organizations can gain valuable insights into attack strategies and tools. These insights can then be used to bolster real network defenses preemptively.

Moreover, advancements in natural language processing (NLP) are significantly impacting the cybersecurity domain. NLP algorithms can analyze and interpret human language with great accuracy, making them perfect for combing through vast amounts of text data to identify potential security threats. For instance, NLP-powered tools can monitor social media, forums, and dark web marketplaces to detect chatter about new vulnerabilities or planned cyber attacks, offering timely intelligence that can be acted upon to prevent breaches.

Robotic Process Automation (RPA) is another front where AI is making its mark. RPA involves automating repetitive tasks that are usually performed by humans. In cybersecurity, RPA can handle tasks like log monitoring, compliance checks, and patch management, freeing up human analysts to focus on more complex problems. When coupled with AI, RPA can even adapt to new threats in real-time, making cybersecurity defenses more dynamic and responsive.

The integration of AI with the Internet of Things (IoT) is also a critical area of focus. IoT devices are proliferating rapidly, from smart homes to industrial systems, and each device represents a potential entry point for cyber attacks. By using AI to monitor and manage these devices, we can achieve a higher level of security. AI can predict potential vulnerabilities, automate the application of security patches, and even isolate compromised devices to prevent them from affecting the entire network.

Finally, the ongoing development of AI-controlled Unmanned Aerial Vehicles (UAVs) or drones presents both challenges and opportunities in cybersecurity. These drones can be used for surveillance and threat detection, providing a mobile and flexible platform for monitoring large areas or hard-to-reach locations. On the flip side, drones can also be exploited by malicious actors for espionage or delivery of payloads to disrupt critical infrastructure. Developing robust countermeasures against these threats is an essential part of future AI-driven cybersecurity strategies.

It's clear that the confluence of these emerging technologies will significantly impact the cybersecurity landscape. While they bring incredible advancements, they also introduce new challenges that need innovative solutions. Staying ahead in the cybersecurity game will require not just implementing these technologies but continuously evolving them to meet emerging threats. As we move forward, the intersection of AI with other advanced technologies promises to offer a dynamic and robust framework for defending our digital world.

Future Trends

Artificial Intelligence (AI) is set to revolutionize cybersecurity in ways that are both promising and complex. We're at the intersection of unprecedented technological innovation and increasingly sophisticated cyber threats. As we look ahead, several key trends emerge that could significantly shape the future landscape of AI in cybersecurity.

One of the most transformative trends is the evolution of **autonomous cybersecurity systems**. These systems could operate with minimal human intervention, dynamically responding to threats in real-time. While current AI systems often require human oversight for decision-making, future iterations might become increasingly self-sufficient. By leveraging machine learning (ML) algorithms that can continuously adapt and learn from each cyber event, these systems promise a leap in defensive capabilities.

Another pivotal trend is the integration of AI with *internet of things (IoT) security*. As IoT devices proliferate across both consumer and industrial sectors, they create a vastly expanded attack surface. Conventional methods struggle to scale with the sheer volume and diversity of connected devices. AI offers a pathway to effectively monitor, analyze, and secure this complex ecosystem. Sophisticated AI models can identify and mitigate potential vulnerabilities before they are exploited, ensuring a more resilient IoT infrastructure.

AI-driven *predictive analytics* is another area likely to see significant advancements. By analyzing vast amounts of data, AI can identify patterns and predict potential security incidents with high accuracy. Imagine a future where security teams can pre-emptively address threats before they manifest, reducing the window for attackers to exploit vulnerabilities. Although still in their nascent stages, predictive models could soon become an indispensable tool for cybersecurity professionals.

We must also consider the advancements in **biometric security systems**. AI-enhanced biometric verification techniques, such as facial recognition, voice identification, and even behavioral biometrics, are steadily improving. While these systems provide enhanced security, they also introduce new ethical and privacy challenges. Balancing effectiveness with ethical considerations will be crucial for future developments in this area.

Moreover, the future will likely see further refinement of **natural language processing (NLP)** for cybersecurity applications. NLP can already parse through massive volumes of text data, such as threat intelligence reports, phishing emails, and dark web communications. Future iterations of NLP could offer even more nuanced understandings and actionable insights, making it an invaluable tool for preemptively identifying cyber threats.

Federated learning represents another intriguing trend. Unlike traditional ML, which requires centralizing data for training models, federated learning allows machines to learn collaboratively without sharing sensitive data. This approach enhances data privacy and can be particularly beneficial for sectors like healthcare and finance, where data sensitivity is paramount. The implications for cybersecurity are profound, as it allows for cross-organization learning of threat patterns without compromising individual data security.

The advent of *quantum computing* poses both a threat and a potential boon for cybersecurity. Quantum computers have the ability to break traditional encryption methods, posing significant risks. However, they also offer the possibility of quantum-resistant algorithms that could fortify security measures. Future AI systems will need to integrate quantum computing technologies, both to harness their defensive capabilities and to guard against their offensive potential.

As cyber threats grow more sophisticated, the notion of **cybersecurity mesh architecture** becomes increasingly relevant. This framework advocates a more modular and flexible approach to security, where different nodes within a network can autonomously manage their own security guidelines while still collaborating with the broader network. AI will be integral in orchestrating these decentralized security frameworks, ensuring cohesion and comprehensive protection.

Human-AI collaboration is expected to become more seamless and integrated. While AI can handle vast data analysis and pattern recognition, human intuition and contextual understanding remain invaluable. Future trends will likely see AI systems designed to work more synergistically with human operators, augmenting their capabilities rather than replacing them. This collaborative approach can facilitate more effective threat detection, response, and mitigation.

The rise of **explainable AI (XAI)** is also on the horizon. Unlike traditional AI models, which often operate as "black boxes," XAI aims to make AI decision-making processes more transparent and understandable. This is especially pertinent in cybersecurity, where understanding the rationale behind AI-driven decisions can help in fine-tuning defenses and gaining trust from stakeholders.

Lastly, we should anticipate the continuous evolution of *AI-based deception technologies*. These technologies deploy decoys and honeypots to mislead attackers, gathering intelligence on their tactics and intentions. Enhanced by AI, these systems will become more sophisticated, effectively simulating real assets and enticing cybercriminals into revealing their strategies.

In summary, the future of AI in cybersecurity is teeming with potential. Autonomous systems, IoT integration, predictive analytics, and advancements in biometrics and NLP are set to redefine the sector. The evolutionary trajectories of federated learning and quantum computing further illustrate the dynamic interplay between emerging technologies and cybersecurity imperatives. Meanwhile, explainable AI and AI-driven deception highlight the ongoing efforts to improve transparency and tactical responses. Human-AI collaboration will eventually lay the foundation for a more robust, resilient, and adaptive cybersecurity landscape. As we move forward, these trends will not only address current challenges but also prepare us for the unseen threats of tomorrow.

Preparing for Tomorrow's Threats

As we propel into an era profoundly shaped by technology, the landscape of cyber threats is evolving with unprecedented speed. Traditionally, cybersecurity has always played a game of catch-up, reacting to new threats as they emerge. The escalating complexity and sophistication of cyber attacks necessitate a paradigm shift. Instead of merely reacting to incidents, we must systematically anticipate and prepare for future threats. This is where the transformative power of Artificial Intelligence (AI) comes into play.

The integration of AI into cybersecurity is not just a technological enhancement but a strategic imperative. AI's ability to analyze vast amounts of data in real-time allows for a predictive approach to cybersecurity. By identifying patterns, anomalies, and potential vulnerabilities before they are exploited, AI transforms the defensive measures from reactive shields into proactive fortresses.

Consider, for instance, the capabilities of machine learning algorithms. These systems excel at recognizing patterns within enormous datasets that would be infeasible for human analysts to process. This isn't just about catching the attacks in progress but preventing them from ever occurring. By understanding the behavioral patterns of malicious activities, AI can forecast potential attack vectors and initiate countermeasures autonomously.

Yet, the preparation for tomorrow's threats extends beyond mere technological advancements. A significant aspect involves cultivating a robust and dynamic cybersecurity culture. Professionals must continuously upgrade their skills and adapt to the ever-changing threat landscape. The reliance on AI in cybersecurity necessitates that the workforce becomes proficient in both cybersecurity fundamentals and AI technologies. Comprehensive training programs and certifications focusing on these dual competencies are essential.

Moreover, there's a pressing need for international cooperation. Cyber threats do not respect geographical boundaries, and a fragmented approach to cyber defense undermines collective security. A unified global strategy that leverages AI can create more resilient defense mechanisms. Sharing intelligence, best practices, and even AI models across borders can empower nations to better predict and fend off cyber threats.

In the quest to prepare for future threats, investment in research and development (R&D) cannot be overstated. The cybersecurity industry must continually innovate to stay ahead of malicious actors who are increasingly using AI for malicious purposes. This includes developing advanced AI algorithms specifically tailored for identifying and countering AI-driven cyber attacks, ensuring that defensive measures remain at the cutting edge.

One promising frontier is the deployment of AI in the field of automated response systems. Unlike traditional incident response mechanisms that may take minutes to hours to react, AI-driven response systems operate in real-time, effectively neutralizing threats as they are detected. These systems not only minimize damage but also provide detailed insights for further fortification of the cybersecurity framework.

Preparing for tomorrow's threats also means understanding the ethical implications of AI deployment in cybersecurity. As AI systems become more integrated into our defense mechanisms, ensuring that these systems are fair, unbiased, and respect privacy is crucial. The creation of ethical guidelines and stringent oversight mechanisms will be vital in maintaining public trust and the integrity of cybersecurity efforts.

Additionally, the regulatory environment will play a significant role. Governments and regulatory bodies must adapt to the rapid advancements in AI and cybersecurity. Forward-thinking policies that promote innovation while safeguarding against abuses are essential. By establishing clear legal frameworks, we can ensure that AI is used responsibly and effectively in the fight against cyber threats.

Ahead of us is a future where AI will no longer be an auxiliary tool but the cornerstone of cybersecurity strategies. Organizations need to envision and build infrastructures that support this evolution. This includes integrating AI into every layer of their cybersecurity architecture, from endpoint protection to network security, ensuring a seamless and robust defensive posture.

The danger of standing still in a rapidly evolving threat environment cannot be overstated. As cyber criminals get smarter and their attacks more sophisticated, our response must be equally agile and forward-thinking. The investments in AI and cybersecurity today are the bulwarks of our digital society tomorrow.

In conclusion, the preparation for tomorrow's threats is a multifaceted endeavor. It encompasses technological innovation, continuous education, international collaboration, ethical compliance, and strategic foresight. By harnessing the power of AI, we transform the way we approach cybersecurity – from reactive responses to predictive, proactive defense mechanisms. The future of AI in cybersecurity holds vast potential, and our readiness to embrace it will define our defense capabilities in the years to come.

Conclusion

As we draw this exploration of artificial intelligence in cybersecurity to a close, it's essential to recognize the monumental changes and challenges that lie ahead. The confluence of AI and cybersecurity is not merely a technological shift but a paradigm transformation that will redefine the digital defense landscape. Through our chapters, we've taken a journey from understanding the nascent stages of AI integration in cybersecurity to envisioning the future where AI stands as a sentinel against increasingly sophisticated threats.

Artificial Intelligence has already begun to reshape how we approach digital defense. Early applications, focusing on anomaly detection and automated responses, have evolved to encompass advanced threat prediction and proactive defense measures. AI's capability to analyze vast amounts of data in real-time empowers cybersecurity professionals to stay ahead of cybercriminals, whose methods grow more elusive and dangerous by the day. However, it is paramount to understand that AI is not an infallible solution but a powerful tool that complements human expertise.

One of the pivotal themes that emerged throughout our discussion is the critical importance of data. In the realm of cybersecurity, data is both a blessing and a challenge. While it provides the raw material for AI algorithms to learn and adapt, it also presents significant hurdles in terms of management, privacy, and ethical considerations. The ability to balance data utility with data protection will be a cornerstone of effective AI-driven cybersecurity strategies.

The nuanced role of AI in threat detection and prevention further underscores its transformative potential. By leveraging machine learning, deep learning, and natural language processing, AI systems can discern patterns and anomalies that might escape even the most vigilant human eyes. This capability extends to real-time monitoring, behavior analysis, and intrusion detection, making it possible to mitigate risks before they escalate into full-blown incidents. Yet, this technological prowess must be paired with robust ethical frameworks to ensure fairness and bias mitigation.

Incident response has also seen significant advancements thanks to AI. Automated incident response systems streamline what has traditionally been a reactive and time-consuming process. AI-driven forensics and crisis management tools ensure that organizations can quickly identify, isolate, and neutralize threats. This swift action is vital in minimizing damage and maintaining operational continuity. However, the reliance on AI for such critical tasks also necessitates stringent testing and validation to prevent false positives and negatives.

Cloud security, another pressing area in modern cybersecurity, has found an ally in AI. As businesses migrate more operations to the cloud, the threat landscape expands, necessitating innovative defenses. AI offers solutions tailored to the unique vulnerabilities of cloud environments, from detecting unauthorized access to predicting potential breaches. Yet, the dynamic nature of the cloud demands continuous vigilance and adaptation from AI systems to stay effective.

The future of AI in cybersecurity is undeniably promising, but it is also fraught with challenges that require careful navigation. Emerging technologies will introduce new capabilities, but they will also bring new vulnerabilities. Preparing for tomorrow's threats will require a forward-thinking approach that embraces innovation while remaining grounded in solid, ethical practices. As we look forward, the collaboration between technologists, policymakers, and cybersecurity professionals will be crucial in shaping a secure digital future.

We can't ignore the ethical dimensions and regulatory frameworks that must evolve alongside these technological advancements. AI's role in cybersecurity introduces complex questions around privacy, bias, and societal impact. Ensuring that AI applications are developed and deployed responsibly will be key to maintaining public trust and achieving long-term success in digital defense. Regulatory and legal aspects will need to keep pace with technological developments, offering guidelines that protect both innovation and individual rights.

To encapsulate, the integration of AI into cybersecurity is not merely a continuation of existing practices but a catalyst for revolutionary change. Through sophisticated algorithms, unparalleled data processing capabilities, and proactive defense mechanisms, AI has made it possible to anticipate and neutralize threats with unprecedented efficiency. Yet, this powerful tool comes with its own set of challenges, emphasizing the need for a balanced approach that combines technological innovation with ethical responsibility and human oversight.

As we conclude, it is worth reflecting on the journey we have embarked upon. From the early days of basic anomaly detection to the sophisticated AI-driven ecosystems of today, the road has been marked by rapid advancements and complex challenges. The lessons learned and the successes achieved point to a future where AI could become the cornerstone of cybersecurity. However, this future will depend on our ability to harness AI's potential responsibly, ensuring that it serves as a force for good in safeguarding the digital world.

In essence, the evolution of AI in cybersecurity represents both a beacon of promise and a call to action. It demands that we stay informed, adaptable, and vigilant. By doing so, we can ensure that AI not only fortifies our digital defenses but also upholds the ethical standards that protect the very fabric of our society. As we move forward, the collaboration between human ingenuity and artificial intelligence will be the linchpin in securing our digital future.

Appendix A:
Appendix

This appendix serves as a practical resource to supplement the core content of the book, providing readers with essential tools and references to deepen their understanding of how AI is revolutionizing cybersecurity. You will find detailed lists of technical terms, acronyms, and jargon commonly used in the field, alongside concise definitions to ensure clarity. Additionally, this section includes curated links to academic papers, industry reports, and authoritative articles that can serve as further reading material for those interested in exploring specific aspects of AI and cybersecurity in greater depth. For professionals looking to implement or hone AI-driven security measures, a selection of recommended software tools and frameworks is also provided. Altogether, this appendix aims to equip you with the resources needed to navigate the complex landscape of AI in digital defense effectively.

Glossary of Terms

This glossary aims to provide clear, concise definitions for key terms and concepts used throughout the book. Understanding these terms will help enhance your grasp of AI's transformative role in cybersecurity.

Advanced Persistent Threats (APTs): A type of cyber attack where unauthorized users gain access to a system and remain undetected for an extended period.

Anomaly Detection: The process of identifying unusual patterns that do not conform to expected behavior, often used to detect suspicious activities in cybersecurity.

Automated Patch Management: Tools and techniques used to automatically update software systems and applications to fix vulnerabilities.

Behavior Analysis: The study of users' and systems' actions to detect potentially malicious activities.

Big Data: Extremely large datasets that may be analyzed computationally to reveal patterns, trends, and associations, especially relating to human behavior and interactions.

Cloud Security: Measures and technologies designed to protect data, applications, and infrastructure associated with cloud computing.

Crisis Management: Strategies and processes employed to respond effectively to cyber incidents and reduce their impact.

Cybersecurity: The practice of protecting systems, networks, and programs from digital attacks.

Data Collection: The process of gathering and measuring information on targeted variables to answer relevant questions and evaluate outcomes.

Deep Learning: A subset of machine learning involving neural networks with many layers, used to model complex patterns in data.

Ethical AI: The practice of designing and using AI in a manner that values ethical considerations such as fairness, accountability, and transparency.

Intrusion Detection Systems (IDS): Solutions designed to detect unauthorized access or attacks on a network or system.

Machine Learning: A field of artificial intelligence where systems are trained to learn from data and improve their performance over time without being explicitly programmed.

Malware: Malicious software designed to disrupt, damage, or gain unauthorized access to computer systems.

Natural Language Processing (NLP): A field of AI focused on enabling machines to understand, interpret, and respond to human languages.

Phishing: A cyber attack method where attackers trick individuals into revealing personal information by pretending to be trustworthy entities.

Predictive Analytics: Techniques that use historical data to make predictions about future events, often used to identify potential security threats.

Proactive Defense Mechanisms: Strategies that aim to prevent cyber attacks before they happen, rather than reacting to them afterward.

Ransomware: A type of malware that locks users out of their systems or encrypts their data, demanding a ransom for restoration.

Real-Time Monitoring Systems: Systems that continuously analyze data to detect and respond to cyber threats instantly.

This glossary covers the crucial terminology you'll need as you navigate through the book. Each term has been selected to provide you with a foundational understanding of the interplay between AI and cybersecurity.

Additional Resources

While understanding the terminology is crucial, having access to supplementary materials can significantly enhance learning and expertise in the realm of AI-driven cybersecurity. The following resources are curated to provide more in-depth insights, practical knowledge, and up-to-date information.

Books are an excellent starting point for anyone looking to delve deeper. "AI in Cybersecurity" by Leslie F. Sikos offers a comprehensive guide to artificial intelligence applications in digital defense. "Hands-On Machine Learning with Scikit-Learn, Keras, and TensorFlow" by Aurélien Géron is another must-read for those interested in practical machine learning applications. For a broader perspective on AI's impact on cybersecurity, "AI Superpowers" by Kai-Fu Lee discusses the geopolitical implications and future trends.

Online courses offer interactive learning experiences and are highly beneficial for those who prefer a structured learning path. Platforms like Coursera, Udacity, and edX provide specialized courses on AI and cybersecurity. The "AI For Everyone" course by Andrew Ng and the "Cybersecurity Specialization" by the University of Maryland on Coursera are highly recommended. These courses often come with hands-on projects, which are invaluable for practical understanding.

For those who prefer self-paced learning, online articles and white papers can be immensely useful. Websites like arXiv.org and Google Scholar host a plethora of research papers that discuss the latest advancements in AI and cybersecurity. The International Journal of Cybersecurity Intelligence & Cybercrime publishes cutting-edge research and case studies, offering a scholarly perspective on current issues in the field.

Joining specialized forums and online communities can also be very beneficial. Websites like Reddit (particularly subreddits like r/cybersecurity and r/machinelearning), Stack Overflow, and specialized forums such as BleepingComputer Forums, provide a platform for discussion, queries, and sharing personal experiences. These communities often have industry experts who can offer invaluable advice and insights.

Participating in webinars and conferences is another excellent way to stay updated with the latest trends and network with professionals in the field. Events like DEF CON, Black Hat, and the RSA Conference frequently feature sessions on AI in cybersecurity. These conferences provide opportunities to learn directly from experts and connect with peers.

Podcasts are a convenient way to consume information on the go. "Smashing Security" and "Security Now" are two popular cybersecurity podcasts that frequently cover topics related to AI and machine learning. Listening to experts discuss real-world applications and emerging threats can provide practical insights and up-to-date information.

Government and industry reports are also rich sources of information. Publications from the National Institute of Standards and Technology (NIST), the Center for Internet Security (CIS), and the European Union Agency for Cybersecurity (ENISA) often include comprehensive sections on AI and machine learning applications in cybersecurity. These reports can serve as reference materials for best practices and compliance requirements.

Open-source tools and platforms offer practical insights and hands-on experience. Tools like TensorFlow, Keras, and PyTorch are widely used for machine learning and deep learning applications in cybersecurity. GitHub is an excellent repository for finding these tools and other valuable resources, including sample projects and code to study.

Furthermore, subscribing to cybersecurity and AI-focused newsletters can help keep you informed. Newsletters like "The Hacker News," "Dark Reading," and "AI Weekly" aggregate the latest news, research, and developments in the field. They are a quick and efficient way to stay updated.

Finally, industry certifications can boost your credentials and deepen your knowledge. Credentials like Certified Information Systems Security Professional (CISSP), Certified Ethical Hacker (CEH), and Certified Artificial Intelligence Practitioner (CAIP) are highly regarded in the field. These certifications often cover advanced topics in AI and cybersecurity, making them valuable for career advancement.

Incorporating these resources into your study and professional practice will not only enhance your understanding of AI in cybersecurity but also keep you at the forefront of this rapidly evolving field.

Suggested Reading

When delving deeper into the transformation of cybersecurity through artificial intelligence, a curated selection of recommended readings can provide valuable insights and expand your understanding of this evolving domain. This section offers a variety of resources that cover different aspects of AI and cybersecurity, catering to both novices and seasoned professionals.

Firstly, for a foundational grasp of AI and its various techniques, you might want to explore "Artificial Intelligence: A Modern Approach" by Stuart Russell and Peter Norvig. This book lays a comprehensive groundwork, explaining the principles and applications of AI, which can be directly related to cybersecurity strategies covered in Chapter 3 of our book.

Turning our focus to the specifics of cyber threats and the role of AI in addressing them, Bruce Schneier's "Click Here to Kill Everybody: Security and Survival in a Hyper-connected World" is a must-read. Schneier elucidates the vulnerabilities in our current digital landscape and how AI can be a double-edged sword, offering both defense mechanisms and new threats.

For an in-depth understanding of machine learning and deep learning, which are pivotal in developing sophisticated cybersecurity solutions, "Deep Learning" by Ian Goodfellow, Yoshua Bengio, and Aaron Courville is an essential text. This book provides technical insights into the algorithms and models that form the backbone of AI-driven cybersecurity tools.

To explore the application of these AI techniques in real-world scenarios, especially regarding threat detection and prevention, "The Threat Intelligence Handbook" by Chris Poulin and Rebekah Brown bridges the gap between theory and practice. The chapters on developing threat intelligence and using AI for proactive defense align perfectly with Chapters 4 and 5 of our book.

Ethical considerations are also crucial when deploying AI in cybersecurity. "Weapons of Math Destruction" by Cathy O'Neil critically examines the ethical implications and biases inherent in AI systems. This book complements Chapter 10's discussion on the ethical and regulatory challenges we face in this field.

For those interested in the legal and regulatory landscape that governs AI and cybersecurity, "Privacy, Big Data, and the Public Good: Frameworks for Engagement" edited by Julia Lane and Victoria Stodden, offers a thorough analysis of privacy concerns, global regulations, and the future of cyber law, tying in neatly with our Chapter 11.

Looking ahead to future trends, "Prediction Machines: The Simple Economics of Artificial Intelligence" by Ajay Agrawal, Joshua Gans, and Avi Goldfarb provides an economic perspective on how AI can transform various sectors, including cybersecurity. This forward-looking text is harmonized with Chapter 12, which delves into emerging technologies and future threats.

For those who prefer a more narrative-driven exploration, "Future Crimes: Inside the Digital Underground and the Battle for Our Connected World" by Marc Goodman offers an engaging overview of digital risks and innovative countermeasures, drawing relevance to multiple chapters in our book.

Lastly, "Mastering Bitcoin" by Andreas M. Antonopoulos, while primarily about cryptocurrency, includes crucial insights on blockchain technology and its potential role in enhancing cybersecurity. Understanding blockchain can add depth to your knowledge, especially in the context of Secure Cloud Environments discussed in Chapter 8.

These suggested readings are curated to provide a deep and broad comprehension of the integration of AI in cybersecurity. By exploring these resources, you'll be well-equipped to navigate and contribute to the continuously evolving landscape of digital defense.

www.ingramcontent.com/pod-product-compliance
Lightning Source LLC
Chambersburg PA
CBHW051242050326
40689CB00007B/1036